WHERE THERE'S A WILL,
THERE'S A
WAY

PETER FARWELL

ARCHWAY
PUBLISHING

Archway Publishing books may be ordered through booksellers or by contacting:

Archway Publishing
1663 Liberty Drive
Bloomington, IN 47403
www.archwaypublishing.com
844-669-3957

ISBN: 978-1-6657-3108-9 (sc)
ISBN: 978-1-6657-3109-6 (hc)
ISBN: 978-1-6657-3122-5 (e)

Library of Congress Control Number: 2022918090

Print information available on the last page.

Archway Publishing rev. date: 10/10/2022

Contents

This book tells the stories of the entrepreneurs whose imaginations, curiosity, drive, and dogged determination made the personal computer one of the most popular devices ever known and at the center of the digital technology revolution that is affecting all of us.

Why should you read this book?

The digital technology revolution impacts everything we do: how we study and learn, how we work, how we deal with data, how we write, how we communicate, how we make and build relationships, even how we play games. This book will improve your understanding of how the digital technology revolution is changing every aspect of our waking lives. It will improve your ability to take advantage of the dramatic changes the revolution is causing.

Acknowledgments

I would like to express my appreciation for invaluable help from the following:

My wife, Barbara Oakley, for her review and helpful suggestions.

My children, Sandra and David Farwell, for their encouragement.

My good friend, Bob Shute, for his thorough edit.

My good friend, Bruce Jones, for help with technology.

My good friend, John Swinden, for his thorough review and helpful suggestions.

My good friend, Jim Lawson, for his moral support.

About the author

Peter Farwell is a chartered professional accountant and certified financial analyst.

As an early purchaser of an Apple II and an avid user of VisiCalc, Peter is uniquely positioned to write this book.

He is a retired partner of public accounting firm Ernst & Young. He was the leader of the Canadian firm's services to the high-technology industry for fourteen years.

Peter cowrote several studies of the Canadian high-technology industry, including a study of trends in the Canadian software industry, conducted by interviewing the CEOs of Canada's twelve leading software companies. He coordinated the Canadian electronic industry's participation in a four-country, four-industry study of Total Quality Management (TQM) practices.

Peter has written articles and given speeches on aspects of strategic planning and financing for high-technology companies. These included a lecture to the Association of Canadian Venture Capital Companies on the six stages of growth of technology companies, based on a 1972 landmark paper on the subject by Professor Greiner of Harvard University.

In 2012 and 2013, he coauthored three studies of Research In Motion that assess its chances of survival and what changes management must make to do so.

In 2015, he wrote *IBM: Can It Survive?* at a time when there was some doubt about IBM's viability.

In 2018, he wrote *Artificial Intelligence and the Job Market*, which addressed the debate on whether AI would create more jobs than it destroys.

How It All Began

So here we go. Here are the stories of how entrepreneurs brought the personal computer into being and why it has become so integral to our lives.

Our story begins with the invention of the microprocessor, the computer on a chip that became the heart of the personal computer. The microprocessor was created by Robert Noyce and Gordon Moore at Intel.

Robert Noyce

Noyce grew up in Grinnell, Iowa, where he attended Grinnell High School and College. He excelled in science. At college, one of his science teachers, Grant Gale, showed him some of the first transistors produced by Bell Labs. Intrigued, he then went on to MIT, where he did a doctoral program in physics. This is where he met William Shockley and joined his team.

Gordon Moore

Gordon Moore started life in San Francisco and attended San Jose State University. In 1950, he earned a BS degree in chemistry at the University of California, in Berkeley. He also joined William Shockley's team of researchers.

Shockley and the first Transistor

In the 1950s, a team at Bell Labs studied semiconductors and invented the transistor, under the leadership of William Shockley. This work earned Shockley, and his coworkers, the 1956 Nobel Prize in PhysicsThe transistor was constructed of semiconductor material, such as Silicon or Germanium. The Bell labs team discovered that you could change the semiconductor wafer into a conductor, thus creating an on/off switch, the transistor.) Later, Schockley moved to California and set up a new operation, the Shockley Semiconductor Laboratory to pursue the further development of the transistor. But his autocratic management style did not appeal to everyone.

Noyce, Moore at Intel and the microprocessor

In 1957, a team of eight broke away from his company and formed Fairchild Semiconductor. The group included Noyce and Moore, who, in 1968, left Fairchild to form Intel. At Intel, they created the x86 series of microprocessors, which became the core of the personal computer.

The series started with the 4004 microprocessor, which was a 4-bit chip, developed in 1971. This microprocessor was the first commercially produced central processing unit (CPU). It was used in a mathematical calculator. The 4004 had 2,400 transistors. And it was shortly followed by the 8008 chip, with an 8-bit CPU. The 8008 had 3500 transistors. Then, in 1974, the 8008 chip was followed by the 8080 chip, which was a faster 8-bit chip. It had 4500 transistors.

Ed Roberts and the first PC kit

At about this time, Ed Roberts, in Albuquerque, New Mexico, became aware of the Intel 8080 microprocessor. Roberts had formed a company named MITS and designed a computer kit around the Intel 8080 chip. It was featured in the January 1975 issue of *Popular*

Electronics. This kit was called the Altair, after the star of that name. Roberts's company produced and sold them in the thousands. The Altair was the centerpiece of the Homebrew Club's first meeting in 1975. It was here that the personal computer's baton passed to Steve Wozniak and Steve Jobs.

The Homebrew Club

On March 5, 1975, Fred Moore and Gordon French formed a group called the Homebrew Club. It was in the heart of what we now refer to as Silicon Valley, California.[1] These people were interested in building their own computers. Thirty-two people showed up for the first meeting, in Gordon French's garage.

The group also included Bill Gates, Paul Allen, Steve Wozniak, and Steve Jobs.

Jobs, Wozniak and the Apple I PC kit

Both Wozniak and Jobs had been well tutored by their fathers. Job's father, Paul, was pretty much self-trained and worked as a machinist at Spectra-Physics. He made lasers for electronics and medical products. Paul had worked for a car company and learned about electronics, as they were used in cars. He was then able to teach Steve the basics of electronics and the importance of keeping things simple but well constructed.

Wozniak's father was an electrical engineering graduate of Cal Tech. He played with electronic parts at home and taught Steve hands-on familiarity with electronic circuits and constituent components.

---

[1] Silicon Valley is in the Santa Clara Valley, which runs south, from San Francisco along the Pacific coast to San Jose. It includes cities such as Sunnyvale, Palo Alto, Menlo Park, and Cupertino. It is the home of Stanford University.

Steve Jobs attended Homestead High School, in Cupertino, California, where he took an electronics course given by John McCollum. McCollum was a bit of a showman and had an array of tricks, to spur his students on. While taking McCollum's class, Jobs was introduced to Wozniak, who had been a star pupil under McCollum and was five years older than Jobs. In spite of the age difference, they formed a fast friendship, built on their common interest in electronics and music.

One of their first projects together was the construction of a device that could replicate the tones of a telephone. This enabled them to make telephone calls free of charge. They replicated dozens of them and sold them to friends. "It gave us a taste of what we could do with my engineering skills and his vision," said Wozniak.

In 1974, Jobs joined the staff of Atari, the video games manufacturer founded by Nolan Bushnell. One of the games developed by Bushnell was Pong. It was a game played by batting a simulated ping-pong ball against a wall. While at Atari, Jobs, with help from his pal Wozniak, was asked to build a single-player version. This was completed in the incredible span of four days.

Wozniak and the Apple I

After seeing the Altair at first meeting of the Homebrew Club, Wozniak was motivated to build his own computer kit. He built a self-contained personal computer around a microprocessor. It was the computer on a chip being produced by Intel and others about this same time. Wozniak actually chose a chip made by MOS Technologies as the core of his PC. It was less expensive than Intel's.

Shortly thereafter, Apple Computer Corp. was created by Jobs and Wozniak. And the Apple I made its debut. This was a PC built for hobbyists. It was, in fact, just a printed circuit board, built around the MOS Technologies microprocessor. It had no power supply, monitor, or keyboard. Purchasers had to buy them and plug them in. There were no application programs.

Purchasers had to do their own programming, using a version of the Basic Program Language written by Wozniak especially for the Apple I. Fortunately, enough of them (about two hundred) were purchased. Apple Computer was off the ground. It had lots of competition, from Altair and Commodore, and was used only by a small minority of the Homebrew Club members. But it was enough to provide a base for the development of the next big thing, the Apple II.

In making this major leap, Wozniak and Jobs were standing on the shoulders of a number of entrepreneurs, who paved the way to a personal computer. And they were familiar with these entrepreneurs through the Homebrew Club. Walter Isaacson provided the details in his book, *The Innovators*. The story was fairly lengthy and involved a number of entrepreneurs; it's summarized in Appendix G.

Jobs, Wozniak and the Apple II

The Apple II was a phenomenal improvement over the Apple I. Steve Wozniak had been working on it around the time the Apple I had been completed. The Apple II, as they named it, would come in its own molded, plastic case. And it contained its own power supply, keyboard, and monitor. It would produce high-resolution graphics in color. As Wozniak envisioned it, "This would be a matter of efficiency and elegance of design."

The Apple II would be designed around text and graphics that would be embedded in the Apple II's own Dynamic Random-Access Memory (DRAM) system. It was much faster than the Apple I and employed fewer chips in the printed circuit. So it was smaller and less expensive to make. And it was the first personal computer to start up and be ready to use, with its basic operating system burned into its internal memory. It did not have to be booted up by the user, which was a tedious process. It was designed for the average home user, rather than the hobbyists of the Homebrew Club.

Each of the many advances incorporated in the Apple II was a marvel itself. For example, the power supply was extremely innovative. It was developed by Rod Holt, an acquaintance of Steve Jobs. Jobs wanted to have a power supply that didn't need a loud fan to cool it. So Holt built one that switched itself on and off very quickly. This allowed it to operate without heating up much, unlike prior power supplies for computers. Therefore, it required no noisy fan for cooling. In Job's words, "That power supply was as revolutionary as the Apple II logic board."

Bricklin, Frankston and Visicalc

As marvelous and innovative as each of these advances were, they weren't the real key to the Apple II's success. The key was VisiCalc, a software program that ran on the Apple II. VisiCalc was the first spreadsheet program for personal computers.

It was developed by Dan Bricklin and Bob Frankston, founders of Software Arts. It was the first fully interactive, row-and-column financial program that was developed for a personal computer. It propelled the Apple II from being a hobbyist's toy to a useful tool for business.

To understand why it was the key to Apple II's success, let's go back into history, my history, with actuarial computations.

In the summer of 1957, I joined Confederation Life (Confed), a now-defunct Canadian insurance company, as an actuarial summer student. One of my jobs was to gather the data on the most recent year's Canadian mortality records. It was assembled, by hand, from Canadian insurance companies' inputs. I integrated these with the accumulated data from prior years.

The result was a new Canadian mortality table that was right up to date and that could be used for calculating insurance premiums and the company's insurance liability reserves. This work, as I recall, was done using NCR calculating machines; the data was entered on massive handwritten spreadsheets. It took most of the summer.

The next summer found me back at Confed, with the same updating task. But this time, I was using IBM punch card machines, calculators, sorters, and accumulators. This was a little faster, but still took most of the summer as I learned how to use the machines and how to feed in the punched cards without destroying the data.

The third summer, I was back again. This time, Confed had purchased an IBM 705, one of the first mainframe computers. It was a massive machine filled with tubes that could be switched on and off to signal and store information in the binary integer system. In that system, each bit is an electric tube switch that was either on, signifying a "1," or off, signifying a "0," in what has been called machine language; eight bits were combined into a byte that could represent, in the binary system, 256 different data points; in this ASCII language, bytes were used to represent the letters of the alphabet, in both lower- and uppercase, integers, punctuation marks, and mathematical operations such as Add and Subtract; the ASCII language could in turn be used to express any sentence or logical operation. (For a fuller description of the ASCII language and its place in the computer software hierarchy, please see Appendix B, A Hierarchy of Computer Hardware and Software.)

The IBM 705, a significant innovation in its time, was constructed before the advent of the transistor; it generated a huge amount of heat and required an immense cooling system, such that it took up an entire floor in the Confed building (a large multistory office building).

My task that summer was to write, in an Assembler programming language, a program that would do the same mortality table update that I had done in each of the preceding two years. As you can imagine, it would result in very large savings in the effort required to update the mortality tables, and it would have been repeatable each year.

The point of this diversion is that a personal computer that could run an electronic spreadsheet would constitute a giant leap forward from the manual creation of spreadsheets. The calculations could be done more easily, it could be corrected more easily, the data could be stored indefinitely or printed numerous times, and the work could be repeated time and time again in exactly the same way.

This was extremely valuable to actuaries building mortality tables and insurance liability schedules, to accountants creating depreciation and other schedules required to produce audited financial statements, to engineers building tables of specifications for new products and services, to investment analysts tracking stock and portfolio performance, and to many others who required spreadsheet data to do their work. VisiCalc was the first program that did this with the convenience of the personal computer.

Personal computer owners could finally develop and run their own personal spreadsheets, while their compatriots were doing theirs, without tying up the company's mainframe. The result was a giant leap forward in productivity and ease of use. Once people found out what they could do with the Apple II, they flocked to buy them, and sales took off.

There are two other important pieces of Apple's history I would like to address before moving on to the next phase in the PC story.

Mike Markkula

Mike Markkula worked at Intel and made millions on stock options before retiring at about age thirty.

He had kept involved in the technology start-up field as an angel investor and consultant who excelled in strategy, organization, and marketing. Jobs was introduced to him by a venture capitalist, and they hit it off

Markkula encouraged Jobs to write a business plan for Apple, and he agreed to invest if he liked the plan. He ended up providing the company with $250,000 for a one-third interest. This was more than enough funding to launch the Apple II.

Even more importantly, Markkula took over the marketing function for Apple. He wrote his approach to marketing in a one-page memo, "The Apple Marketing Philosophy." It set out three principles that are so good, they bear repeating here as a guide for any high-tech company.

Exude Empathy. Make every effort to understand the needs of your target customers as those customers perceive them. We will come back to this principle later when we discuss the operating approach of Dell Computers. But the key point is that those perceived needs should drive everything your company does.

Focus. Eliminate all the lesser opportunities and put all the company's resources into pursuing its best opportunities, those required to enable it to succeed. This is extremely difficult for an entrepreneur to do but absolutely key to success.

Impute. This awkward word conveys the need to infuse the company's entire operations with the same values as its main products or services. This allows customers and other stakeholders to understand what the company stood for by looking at any part of its operations. If you are introducing an innovative product or service, you must market it in an equally innovative way. This is how you will build trust in your ability to innovate. This mantra has guided Apple's marketing to this day.

Markkula's investment of two hundred and fifty thousand dollars was critical, but his marketing practices were even more significant.

Wozniak's Graphics Capability

The other piece of the business is the graphics capability Wozniak built into the Apple II. It was far superior to that in any other PC at that time and gave Apple a significant competitive advantage. It helped make the Apple II fun and easy to use.

As Wozniak tells it in his autobiography, *iWoz*, he designed the Apple II with a colour graphics capability coded right into its main memory. The Apple II was designed to work with any TV as a monitor. It had game control paddles that could be plugged in, and it had sound. It was also a high-resolution machine. You could program every single pixel on the screen. And it had more CPU memory than its competitors, 48k to start with, and 64k in later versions. (The latter as much as that IBM 705 mainframe that I had to program at Confed in 1959, seventeen years earlier.)

All these features made the Apple II attractive to creators of computer games. As a result, a whole new community of start-ups was formed to write software and build attachments that could run computer games on the Apple II. This was a very competitive market, and it was hard for any company to build much traction in the early days.

Wozniak noted it was VisiCalc that caused the sales of the Apple II to explode, changing the market for personal computers from that of hobbyists playing games to business users who achieved a quantum leap in productivity. "After a couple of months, the business people were something like 90% of the market" he wrote.

Ultimately the Apple II, in its various versions (Apple II+, Apple IIe) sold over 16 million units and put Apple Computer Inc. in the Fortune 500, right in the middle of one of the greatest technology revolutions ever.

The IBM PC

The IBM PC was launched on August 21, 1981, and ushered in a new era for the personal computer. However, compared to the success of the Apple II and its close connection to the use of VisiCalc, the IBM PC story is much more complex and took place more than a decade after its launch.

It is not so much a story of the sales of IBM's PCs as a story of the sales of its clones. The software for the IBM PC, in particular its operating system and word processing software, went through a succession of iterations, which are not well documented, before the IBM PC and clones reached dominance with about 90 percent of the personal computer market in 1992, eleven years after it was launched.

While it is not possible to show the close correlation between the sales of the IBM PC and its word processing software that was present between the sales of the Apple II and VisiCalc, there are some clues to the importance of the word processing software to the acceptance of the IBM PC, particularly in the office. The story unfolded as outlined in the following paragraphs.

IBM's Personal Computer Series

The IBM PC was by no means IBM's first attempt at a personal computer.

By 1981, IBM had produced and marketed a series of machines that it referred to as personal computers.

According to the IBM archives, the origin of a single-user computer goes back to 1973. In that year, IBM produced a working prototype of its 5100 Portable Computer, which allowed users to perform desktop calculating operations, but not with the spreadsheet capability of VisiCalc; there were a limited variety of canned applications, which presumably did not include word processing. In 1983, *PC Magazine* looked back ten years and called this limited-capability machine a "revolutionary concept" because of its single-user capability.

There followed a series of such machines, each with improvements over its predecessors.

The IBM PC

Gates and Allen steal the show

The machine now known as the IBM PC was launched in August of 1981 in a most unusual way.

IBM had been fretting for some time about the creation of a microcomputer for a single user that could operate on a stand-alone basis and perform a multitude of tasks. Other computer manufacturers, such as Apple, Commodore, and Atari, were selling such machines into the business world and eating into IBM's primary market. But IBM had been concerned that such a machine would cannibalize its existing array of business machines and so delayed its own development of a true personal computer.

The growing success of Apple with the aid of VisiCalc forced IBM to change its tune.

To short-circuit the development period, IBM decided to build the IBM PC on the Intel 8080 series of microprocessors, rather than one of its own, and to hire Microsoft to produce the computer's operating system. Further, it decided to make its PC design open so that other manufacturers could clone it without peril. Both these decisions were atypical for IBM, and yet each contributed to the success of the IBM PC in the marketplace.

IBM PC Hardware

First, let's look at the hardware for the IBM PC. The story of PC hardware centers around the work of Intel and the development of the general-purpose microprocessor that became the core of the personal computer.

Intel was formed in July of 1968 by the partnership of Robert Noyce and Gordon Moore, with funding provided by Arthur Rock from a list of about a dozen angel investors prepared to back a new technology idea under a team of superior leaders. Andrew Grove joined Noyce and Moore to form the triumvirate that would lead Intel to a revolution.

Both Noyce and Moore were employees of Fairchild Semiconductor for a decade and had worked on various ideas that led to the development of a general-purpose microprocessor, that became the heart of Intel's offerings.

The Intel microprocessor, called the 4004, was conceived as "a general-purpose logic chip that could follow programming instructions." In 1971, it was first developed for Busicom to control their stand-alone calculator. Under the agreement with Busicom, Intel retained "the rights to the new chip and [was] allowed to license it to other companies for purposes other than making a calculator."

The terms of this deal were critical to the future developments at Intel and ultimately the transfer of strategic corporate power in the PC industry from hardware manufacturers to software developers. The 4004 was soon followed by the Intel 8080 chip. This was the start of a series of innovative chips (the x86 series).

The Intel 8080 was used in the Altair 8800 microcomputer, which is considered by many to be the first true personal computer. The Altair 8800 was developed by MITS and was the primary object of interest at the historic 1975 meeting of the Silicon Valley Homebrew Computing Club. The first programming language for the machine was Microsoft's initial product, Altair BASIC.

The real takeoff of the PC microprocessor at Intel started with the initiative by IBM to create a true personal computer. This initiative started in 1981, when IBM approached Intel to design and manufacture the microprocessor that would be the core of the new IBM PC.

The microprocessor designed by Intel (for this purpose) was the 30826 microprocessor, part of the x86 series that originated with the 4004. This series was the result of continuous improvements in the power of the Intel microprocessor that is now referred to as Moore's law. A listing of the Intel series of microchips is set out in Appendix H.

Moore's Law

Gordon Moore first stated Moore's law in 1965, in response to a request to offer his view of the prospective growth in power of the microchip. He published a paper in which he projected that the power of the microchip would double every year for ten years. Specifically, he stated that he expected the number of transistors that could be placed in a microchip would double every year for the next ten years. (Compounding exponential growth of 100 percent each year.) By doubling the number of transistors on a microchip, Intel could cut the cost of producing the microchip by the same factor of two every year; the processing speed would also double over the same one-year period. It appears to me that Moore was not so much making a forecast as he was setting a goal at which the Intel researchers could aim.

In 1975, he revised this projection to state that the number of transistors that could be placed on a microchip would double every two years. While no exponential growth in the real world can go on forever, the surprising fact is that this doubling every two years was achieved by Intel for more than forty years. The result is that today's chips are many times more powerful, many times more energy efficient, and many times cheaper than the original. It is the exponential growth in the power of the PC, following Moore's law, that has allowed the continuous improvement in the PC, that has provided much of the base for the PC's success over forty years.

PC Software

Now let's look at the PC operating software story.

Operating software manages and controls the operation of a computer.

The group within IBM charged with creating the IBM PC had talked to Gary Kildall, the founder of Digital Research, about using the CP/M operating system he had developed; it had become the microcomputer industry standard by 1980. However, they were unable to reach an agreement, and IBM decided to go with Microsoft to provide both the basic programming language and the operating system for the IBM PC (the latter something Microsoft had never done before).

This part of the story of the PC's operating system can be traced to the formation of the partnership of Bill Gates and Paul Allen. Gates was still in high school at the time. Their interest in the personal computers was piqued by the article in the January 1975 issue of *Popular Electronics* that showed off the Altair computer, a kit that allowed computer hobbyists to put together a machine that could be used to do calculations, store them, and spit them out at the user's command. It could also run computer gaming software.

Gates and Allen quickly realized that an operating system, which controlled the operations of the computer, could be used to dominate the PC market; as a result, it would become much more important than the hardware, which could be commoditized. As a result, most of the profits in the PC industry, they felt, would accrue to the software providers.

The Altair was managed by an operating system called BASIC (Beginners All-purpose Symbolic Instruction Code). The BASIC operating system had been created at Dartmouth to allow nonengineers to write software for the PC.

To seize control of the budding personal computer industry, Gates and Allen became very familiar with BASIC. Later, they learned about more complex operating systems such as COBOL, a system designed to process business transactions.

In 1972, they learned that Intel's 8008 microprocessor, a more powerful upgrade of the 4004, Intel's initial computer on a chip, was being used as the core of the upgraded Altair PC. They decided to write a BASIC operating system for the Intel 8008 being used in the Altair PC.

Gates and Allen convinced Ed Roberts, the CEO of MITS, the inventor and marketer of the Altair, that MITS should sell the Altair with their BASIC operating system software.

In 1975, Gates and Allen entered into an agreement with Roberts to license the BASIC software to MITS for resale with the Altair. The license was for a ten-year period for thirty dollars per copy. But significantly, under the license, Gates and Allen would retain ownership of the software, and MITS was required to make its best efforts to sublicense the software to other PC hardware manufacturers.[2] Gates and Allen foresaw that these provisions would allow them to define the PC market. Thus, they were well prepared when, in 1981, IBM came looking for an operating system for its new PC.

As we have noted, for some time, IBM had been looking at the creation of a general-purpose microcomputer for a single user that could operate on a stand-alone basis and perform a multitude of tasks. IBM was concerned about cannibalizing its existing computer offerings and so perhaps was deliberately slow in launching its own PC. However, the success of Apple with the Apple II and some other PC manufacturers, such as Commodore and Atari, caused IBM to bite the bullet.

Because it had been slow to make the launch decision, IBM set a one-year time limit for the PC development team. This tight deadline caused

---

[2] Ibid.

the team to build their PC on the Intel 8080 series of microprocessors and to look outside for its operating system.

Jack Sams was the member of IBM's PC development team in charge of software. When the decision to create an operating PC in a year was made, Sams realized he would have to subcontract the development of the operating system software. He placed an historic call to Bill Gates.

Gates and Allen were well primed for this call, based on their history of writing operating system software for the Altair and other work in that field.

Gates and Allen were aware that Tom Paterson, working at a small company, Seattle Computer Products, had developed an operating system for the Intel 8008 series of microchips, which Paterson labelled QDOS. When the IBM overture came, Paul Allen quickly bought Paterson's QDOS, for any use, for fifty thousand dollars.

Armed with that purchase, Microsoft entered negotiations with IBM to provide an operating system for the IBM PC, to be known as PC-DOS (Personal Computer-Disk Operating System). While they did not have this software at the start of the negotiation, they were confident they could produce it quickly, by improving the Paterson QDOS system. This they did in eight months, in time for the launch of the IBM PC.

Gates was adamant that the deal with IBM should be similar to the one he had negotiated earlier with Tom Roberts at MITS for BASIC, that is that Microsoft would retain ownership of the operating system, and beyond that, that Microsoft's license with IBM would be nonexclusive, so Microsoft could license the same software under the name MS-DOS to anyone else. Under this deal, Microsoft would keep control of the source code, so only it could make changes to the software, thus retaining control over its future development. Thus, the stage was set for Microsoft's dominance of PC operating systems.

The IBM PC was launched in 1981. While it met with immediate success, the takeoff was slow, compared to the success of the Apple II. The IBM PC and its clones were aimed principally at a much larger market, the office market. To appeal to this market, IBM relied principally on word processing software, which was becoming available in the late 1970s and 1980s.

Word Processing Software

IBM PCs and clones were not the instant success we've come to expect in the smartphone and tablet computer markets. In the first year, market acceptance was slow, despite IBM's longstanding leadership in serving the business market. In large part, this was deliberate. IBM did not want to have the PC take sales from its existing array of computer equipment for the business office. For example, IBM chose EasyWriter as the word processor for the IBM PC.[3]

EasyWriter

Easy Writer was initially written by John Draper for the Apple II, probably in 1977. It was a simple word processor. EasyWriter Professional launched in 1980, competing against software from Wang, DEC, and IBM. EasyWriter "was the only package, at the time, to display text on the screen exactly as it would appear on the printed page"[4] (perhaps the first word processor to achieve WYSIWYG, "what you see is what you get"). *Personal Computing* magazine judged it the best of the bunch in January 1981.

However, it had some serious limitations, including the fact that it used a nonstandard disk operating system. Nevertheless, when IBM was

---

[3] Wikipedia on the IBM PC.
[4] *IEEE Annals of the History of Computing*, October-December 2006.

unable to cut a deal with Seymour Rubinstein of MicroPro (see below), it opted to go with EasyWriter, even though the version to run on the IBM PC was not ready, and they had to use an earlier version. This turned into a disaster. A typical commentary was a *PC Magazine* article reviewing it titled "The Not-So-Easy Writer."

Seymour Rubenstein and Wordstar

At that time (1981), the dominant word processor was MicroPro's WordStar. WordStar ran on the CP/M operating system, was the industry leader in 1978 and became the first of a series of three serial monopolies of word processing software. Seymour Rubinstein established MicroPro in 1978 and teamed up with a CP/M programmer, John Barnaby, who wrote the program for WordStar. It incorporated the best features of existing WP software running on minicomputers but ran on personal computers using CP/M.[5]

It was Rubinstein's goal to get a larger share of the market, as the lead part of a software suite aimed at the growing microcomputer industry.

WordStar launched in June of 1979, with a lot of innovative features, and over the next five years became the runaway leader in word processing software, hitting its peak in 1984. A keynote of particular interest to us is the following observation in the IEEE article:

> Rubinstein believes that WordStar provided a reason for someone ... to buy a [microcomputer], because WordStar ... made the computer functional and useful immediately. To Rubinstein, WordStar was the first "killer application" because of its dominance of the marketplace and its millions of dollars in sales.[6]

However, MicroPro and WordStar fell on hard times as a result of several events in 1984, the most serious of which was a heart attack

---

5 Ibid.
6 Ibid.

suffered by Rubinstein. Its place as the industry leader was taken by the second serial word processing monopoly, WordPerfect, running on PC-DOS and MS-DOS.

WordPerfect

WordPerfect was the leading WP software from 1984 to about 1990.

WordPerfect was originally written for a Data General minicomputer in 1979. The authors incorporated a company, Satellite Systems International, and sold it under the name WordPerfect. A version that ran on PC-DOS was produced in 1982. The software was a clear improvement on WordStar, with automatic paragraph numbers and automatic numbering and placement of footnotes.

In 1989, WordPerfect 5.1 for PC-DOS was released with even more useful features. These included Apple Macintosh-style pull-down menus and support for tables.

"Some would argue that this version of WordPerfect is still the best Word Processor in the Business."[7]

The IBM PC/2

In 1987, IBM initiated an effort to seize back control of the PC market by introducing the PC/2, with features that were an advance over the original IBM PC and a new operating system, developed with Microsoft.

However, this strategy backfired on IBM, and in 1989, Microsoft came out with Windows, its own new operating system for PCs.

Windows incorporated a graphic user interface (GUI) and provided an intuitive multitasking environment for computers. The main components of the GUI were developed at Xerox Palo Alto Research Center, but it was Steve Jobs at Apple who realized the significance of it, "how friendly computer screens would become by using metaphors that people already understand such as that of documents on a desktop."

---

[7] Ibid.

The GUI replaced instructions in the form of typed lines of text, used by MS-DOS, with graphic objects on the computer screen that could be manipulated by users to guide the computer, usually by means of a mouse. Jobs had Apple incorporate the GUI in its offering of the Macintosh line of personal computers starting in 1984. Apple added a number of improvements, such as a fixed menu bar, drop-down menus, and a trash can.

Gates was aware of this development at Apple because he was busy writing the operating system software for the Apple Macintosh. He realized its power and knew that the GUI had been developed at Xerox PARC and was freely available to others to use as they saw fit. So it became a part of the first Windows operating system, Windows 1.0.

Gates announced the release of Windows in 1985, well after the Macintosh had come out, but the fact that IBM PCs and its clones dominated the market ensured that Windows would be a market leader.

Windows 1.0 was not an immediate runaway success. At about the same time, Microsoft released its word processing software, Word, which was compatible with Windows. We have made the case that the success of Word was a key factor in the eventual success of Windows, but this didn't happen immediately, as businesses were slow to capitalize on the productivity advantages of Word.

Microsoft and Word

In 1989, Microsoft launched Windows for the IBM PC and clones market and along with it, Word for Windows (the third and present word processing serial monopolist). As noted above, Windows became the dominant operating system for the IBM PC and clones and by 1996 had achieved a market share of close to 90 percent. Microsoft's monopoly power in the PC marketplace was undoubtedly a key factor in the runaway success of Windows 1989 and later versions. But it is interesting to note that this coincides with the success of Word in this marketplace at about the same time. Each software system went through a number of iterations before taking off, but these happened at roughly the same time. It is our thesis that this was more than a coincidence and that the arrival of a solid word processing package, Word, contributed to the strength of Windows and was a major contributor to the rapid growth of the PC market that occurred after 1989.

Why was word processing so important to the popularity of the personal computer? It may seem like a silly question today when PCs are so pervasive; everyone has one, many more than one. But in the 1970s and 1980s, it was a question technology people puzzled over.

Apple had shown that PCs could be useful as more than a hobbyist's toy or a machine to play simple games on, with the help of a colour graphics capability and the VisiCalc software that broadened the user market to include spreadsheet users: accountants, engineers, architects, sales and marketing people, and the like.

The IBM PC was targeted at a much bigger market: the office market. To make sales in that market, IBM and clone manufacturers touted the improvement in efficiencies that were possible. Many companies took that for granted and bought tons of the machines, but in fact, it was over a decade after the launch of the IBM PC before most companies began to realize the major productivity improvements that the suppliers had foreseen. This sea change in productivity occurred around the typing function.

In the old days (up to 1980), letters, documents, and the like, were produced by a process that involved the author dictating the document to a secretary who took shorthand (at a later stage, to a tape recorder). The secretary, or typing pool, took the dictation and typed it on a variety of typewriters that became more sophisticated as time passed. The typed document was returned to the author, who corrected it, changed it, and returned it to the typist, who corrected the original by a process of literal cut-and-paste, white-outs, and retypes, or in severe cases retyping the entire document. After another round of proofreading, the document was printed, circulated, and filed. Believe it or not, this tedious process was still being followed by many companies into the late 1980s and in some cases the early 1990s. Finally, after the arrival of decent operating systems, PC-DOS followed by Windows, and decent word processing software, WordPerfect, followed by Word, companies began to change the process of creating documents.

A new generation of authors learned to type their own documents on their PCs, do their own corrections, and initiate their own printing, circulation, and storage. The job of the secretary was changed drastically, as typing was no longer their main function; their numbers were greatly reduced, and their title was often changed to administrative assistant. Where many authors had their own secretary under the old process, the great majority came to share administrative assistants, who could now look after several authors. Thus, the efficiencies in the office market, touted earlier by the PC manufacturers, were finally being realized. But in many cases, it was in the early 1990s that this move forward occurred. And of course, it was the word processing software, WordPerfect running on DOS, and from 1989 Microsoft's Word running on Windows, that made this possible. Over the ten-plus years after 1981, the PC became pervasive in the office market.

Word processing software also contributed significantly to the growth of PCs in the home market, where as Seymour Rubenstein foresaw, it gave the man or woman in the home, something really useful and general purpose to do with the PC, something word processing software made easy to do: type letters and documents.

In summary, just as VisiCalc spreadsheet software led to a large expansion in the market for PCs in the early 1980s, word processing software was a major contributor to the next large expansion in the personal computer market, both in the office and in the home, that occurred in the late 1980s and early 1990s. Of course, there was much other software created for the PC market; for example, database programs, particularly relational database managers popularized by Oracle and Terra Data; presentation programs such as PowerPoint; and many others. But each of these was aimed at and used by only a part of the office market. The really pervasive use was word processing.

Windows 1.0 was the first in a succession of operating systems that allowed Microsoft to maintain its dominance in that field to present times. By 1996, Microsoft had obtained a 90 percent market share in PC operating systems.

In 1990, Windows 3.0 was released with an improved program manager and a new icon system that provided a better user interface, a new file manager, support for sixteen colors, and greater speed and reliability.[8] Windows 3.0 was well received and sold over 2 million copies in half a year.[9]

In 1995, Windows 95 was released with greatly improved user-friendliness, because of the use of an object-oriented user interface. It also introduced the Start menu and Taskbar to replace the program manager. It too was well accepted.

A further series of Windows offerings followed. This series incorporated enough improvements over the years to keep Windows as the dominant PC operating system. They are summarized in Appendix F: A History of PC Operating Software.

As we look at the personal computer market today, we can see that Microsoft's Windows is the dominant operating system (83 percent); it runs on almost all IBM PCs. Competing operating systems are primarily the MacOS (11 percent) that runs on the Apple Macintosh, the first PC with a graphic user interface, and Linux (2 percent), a free operating system used primarily on mainframe and supercomputers, but also on some PCs.[1]

---

[8] *Thought Magazine.*
[9] Wikipedia.

The Graphic User Interface

A history of the personal computer would not be complete without a fuller reference to the GUI, since it amounted to as much of a revolution in the way we use computers as any other innovation. In essence, a GUI is software that allows a user to display and manipulate graphic objects on the computer and to use these manipulations as the main way of operating the computer, usually by means of a mouse. Previously, operating systems used Command Line Interfaces (CLIs), typed lines of text; this was the system used by MS-DOS and all predecessors.

While the history of the GUI can be traced farther back, we will start our commentary with the work at Xerox Palo Alto Research Center (PARC). One of PARC's goals was humanizing computers. It developed the first usable GUI for its Alto computer in 1974.

Steve Jobs was familiar with the work at PARC and discovered that the GUI was not patent protected. He decided to incorporate it in his next line of computers, the Macintosh line, released in 1984. Apple included several improvements in its version of the GUI, including developing overlapping windows (a portion of the computer's monitor screen that operated independently from the rest of the screen) and icons (graphic images that could be used to initiate actions by the computer).

These innovations were quickly adopted by most other PC operating systems developers and in many other devices as well. Microsoft incorporated the GUI in its first version of Windows, Windows 1.0, in

1985. Microsoft gradually improved its version of the GUI, and by 1995, in Windows 95, it was a high-quality offering.[10]

Steve Jobs and the MacIntosh

We have not otherwise commented on the Macintosh, because, while it was an immense success for Apple, by the time it was introduced, the IBM PC (and clones) had taken over the personal computer business market. But we will show the power of the use of graphics by showing our short history in graphic form against a backdrop of the history of personal computer unit sales in two graphics. The first graph, Appendix A, shows the history of the first twenty years of the personal computer, from its inception in 1975 to 1994, the pre-internet era.[11] The second graph, Appendix C, shows the history from the first commercial use of the internet to 2012.[12] Later, we will discuss the remarkable history of Apple that followed after the development of the Apple I and II and the Macintosh.

---

[10] https://www.Linfo.org/gui.html
[11] From data extracted from Ars Technica article.
[12] From Wikipedia data from the Gartner Group.

The Next Great Leap Forward

This sets the scene for the next great leap forward, the conversion of the PC from being primarily a workstation to being primarily a communication device. The driver in this case was the arrival of the internet and the World Wide Web (WWW). We are going to tell this part of the story by looking at Dell Computers, now Dell Inc., since Dell was both an instrument of the growth in PCs that occurred because of the arrival of the internet and one of the principal beneficiaries.

Michael Dell and Dell Computers[13]

I first encountered Michael Dell in 1990 at a high-tech conference in San Francisco. It was a well-established two-day event at which young technology companies, including start-ups hoping to attract funding or partnerships, would show their new ideas, products, and services to an audience of venture capitalists and established tech companies. The conference also had some luminaries who presented a series of keynote speeches. Michael Dell was one of the latter, slated as the keynote speaker before lunch on the first day. Dell's subject that year was, What's Wrong with the Personal Computer? He was assigned a time slot with about forty-five minutes and a half-hour question period to follow.

---

[13] Wikipedia, Michael Dell.

Dell delivered eight zingers on what was wrong with the PC industry, each one representing a significant business opportunity. He delivered them all in eight minutes and sat down. The audience was so stunned that there were few questions, and the conference organizers had to start the lunch break about an hour early. As for me, on returning home and doing a bit of research on Dell Computers, I bought a few shares of the company.

Dell had gone public in 1988 and had immediate success in selling PCs, but this success was not showing up much on the bottom line, and so the company's shares drifted along without much movement either way until about 1992. In that year, the price moved up a bit, and Dell did a three-for-two share-split while maintaining its price. The share price stumbled along at the new level for several more years and then took off like a rocket in 1995. Between 1992 and 1999, the stock was split two-for-one six times, 96 times the stock at Dell's initial public offering (IPO), and in 2000, the split stock hit an all-time high of $58 per split share.

How did Michael Dell and company generate all this wealth? Dell started his business to manufacture and sell personal computers in innovative ways in 1984, when he was still at school. The business experienced some success, and in 1988, it went public, raised $30 million, and attained a market value of $85 million.

By that time, Dell was well known for its distinctive direct sales approach. Dell sold its PC directly to its customers, not using the established retail and wholesale channels employed by others. This approach enabled it to learn quickly exactly what its customers wanted and to modify what it was selling to meet these needs more quickly than any other PC vendor. (Incidentally, this is still the company's mantra to this day, as illustrated by this quote from the home page of the Dell website: "From unconventional PC start-up to global technology leader, the common thread in Dell's heritage is an unwavering commitment to the customer.")

But the whole story of Dell's success goes much deeper than this direct contact with customers. Dell's management philosophy is grounded in the Total Quality Management (TQM) system, whose principal originator was W. Edwards Deming, an American physicist who developed the TQM methodology in the 1930s, '40s, and '50s. Prior to TQM, manufacturers operated on the assumption that there were definite trade-offs among the manufacturing factors: time, quality, and cost. If you tried to make improvements in one of these three factors, it could only be done at the expense of the other two. Deming changed that.

The essence of Deming's TQM was twofold: (1) define quality as the needs of the customer and put in place a system to identify these needs; and (2) put in place a businesswide process to continuously improve the ability of the business to meet those needs.

The definition of quality was novel and depended on the business being in close touch with its customers, communicating with those customers on a continuous basis and applying this knowledge to provide the business with its strategic direction. This, of course, is exactly what Michael Dell did in setting up his PC business to sell directly to customers.

The second part of Deming's TQM was perhaps more challenging. It involved the entire operations of the business and the entire management structure. In the ideal, each and every function of the business had to be optimized with respect to delivering to the needs of the function's customers within the business. Thus, for example, the accounting function had to keep the accounts, and it also had to provide accounting information to the parts of the business that needed it to perform their function, and so on down to the factory workers on the manufacturing line and the sales staff selling the product or services to the ultimate customers.

Another objective of the continuous improvement process was to eliminate waste by identifying the causes of waste: poor design, poor processes, or poor workmanship, as early as possible to reduce waste as quickly and cheaply as possible. The TQM system thus could allow the achievement of simultaneous improvements in quality, what the customer needs; time, how long it takes to deliver products and processes that meet those needs; and costs, how much it costs to deliver those products and processes. For the businesses that implemented this system, the result was a significant competitive advantage that, because of the continuous improvement methodology, grew over time.

Deming, and others, tried to get American companies to adopt this approach but found few takers. However, because of several visits to Japan after the World War II, he found that Japanese manufacturers welcomed him and his ideas with open arms. Their industries had been destroyed during the war, and they were anxious to rebuild them in a way that would allow them to compete effectively against world competition. The result is history that is still playing out. Using TQM, or variations of it, Japanese automotive and electronics companies became world leaders, something still true to this day.

One of the intriguing questions is why American businesses were not quicker to adopt the TQM way. There are undoubtedly several reasons: The methods were revolutionary and perhaps required a huge leap of faith; they involved the application of statistical methods pioneered by Deming that had not been taught much in engineering classes of the day and so required a lot of retraining in a field that to this day continues to be difficult to master; but perhaps most of all, it entailed turning the organization chart upside down so that at each level, managers did not boss their employees around but served them by doing their best to ensure the employees had the required training, to ensure the employees had the required tools and equipment, and to ensure the employees were performing the right jobs. The idea that managers were to serve the people reporting to them rather than the next level up was revolutionary and contrary to every system of management up to that time. It went against the grain of managers from the lowest levels to the CEOs, and most found it difficult if not impossible to switch.

The following illustration of the difficulties traditionally managed companies were faced with TQM was told to me by Raymond Royer, the president of Bombardier, a world-class Canadian transportation equipment company. Royer was a bright, soft-spoken accountant, who was thoroughly committed to the TQM way. Shortly after Bombardier took over the Irish aerospace company, Short Brothers PLC ("Shorts"), Royer visited the Shorts plant in Belfast, Northern Ireland, and was given a full tour, which wound up in the executive dining room. On the tour, he was shown four separate dining facilities: the cafeteria for the factory workers, a dining room for the factory managers, a dining room for the office personnel, and finally, the executive dining room for the senior officers and directors of the company.

During the meal in the executive dining room, Royer passed on the following observation to his hosts, in his low-key way: "At Bombardier, we all eat in the cafeteria." Shorts got the message, and a few months later, on his next visit, Royer found everyone eating in the cafeteria, where the food was very good.

In contrast to most North American companies, the Japanese were starting pretty much from scratch and needed to be different, so they adopted TQM and used it to produce some of the new world leaders in manufacturing. Of course, American companies caught on, and the more progressive adopted some or all of the TQM approach. The American car companies were forced to do this in the 1980s to try to meet the Japanese competition. And Michael Dell was one of the high-tech leaders who saw the merits of the system and built his company on it.

Dell took the TQM philosophy a step further, using a system called "integrated manufacturing." Integrated manufacturing was a management system that was becoming popular in the 1980s and 1990s. It consisted of identifying the business functions that were critical to the success of the business, focusing all effort and energy on optimizing these functions, and outsourcing everything else to a select group of suppliers who were the best in performing the outsourced functions. A key element of a successful integrated manufacturing approach was communications, both among functions inside the business and with the supply chain supplying the outsourced functions. An integrated manufacturing system was designed to keep all the people involved in internal functions, such as final product assembly, and all suppliers fully aware on a real-time basis of where their products were in the supply and manufacturing chain, right through to the ultimate customers. Perhaps more importantly, it would communicate to suppliers where and when their products or services were falling short on quality, time of delivery, and costs. This allowed suppliers to correct any shortcomings as quickly as possible and to minimize rejects and returns. This in turn resulted in meeting customer needs more quickly and with substantial cost savings.

One of the consequences of a smoothly operating integrated manufacturing system was the achievement of just-in-time (JIT) inventories throughout the business and the businesses of its suppliers. JIT required less working capital and was another contributor to the cost savings possible with the system.

Running these TQM and integrated manufacturing systems, Dell became the top performer in the PC business, delivering products that met its customers' needs, on a timely basis, and at industry low costs. For example, Dell became known as the best in the PC business at JIT savings. Dell prospered with steadily increasing sales and profits following its IPO in 1988. However, as previously noted, this prosperity was not much reflected in its share price until 1995, when the share price took off and went on a tear of exponential growth for the next six years.

The Internet and World Wide Web

What happened in 1995? One thing that happened was the start of widespread commercial use of the internet.

The arrival of the internet caused a revolution in how personal computers were used; they became primarily communication devices rather than workstations, a development that exploded sales of PCs. Of course, there were networks of PCs before 1995. Local area networks (LANs) linked computers in an office so they could communicate with one another. Then wide area networks (WANs) proliferated, linking computers from office to office across the country. But generally, these were private networks and only proprietary terminals and PCs, with passwords, could hook into the network.

The internet was something else. It was, and is, a network of computers that eventually spanned the globe, linking any computer that had networking capability to any other such computer, regardless of who owned it or where it was located. How did this happen, and what did it do to the way we use personal computers? (Please refer also to Appendix D: A Hierarchy of Network Hardware and Software, and Appendix E: A Hierarchy of Network Standards.)

The concept of a global network of computers can arguably be traced to the work of J. C. R. Licklider, beginning in 1960. In 1962, Licklider was tasked with the job of creating a network of computers within the US Department of Defense.

In 1969, Robert Taylor headed up a group at the U.S. Department of Defense called the Advanced Research Projects Agency (ARPA) whose aim was to create a network of computers based on the theories developed by Licklider. The network was motivated by the cold war of the time to be decentralized to "enable government researchers to communicate and share information across the country in the aftermath of a nuclear attack." The network they came up with used packet switching, "a rapid store-and-forward network design that divides messages up into arbitrary packets, with routing decisions made per packet." This method of routing was far superior to existing methods and allowed faster communications among computers. Packet switching is still the method used by the internet to this day.

The first ARPANET link using this methodology was established on October 29, 1969, between the University of California, Los Angeles and the Stanford Research Institute (SRI).

Here is a quote from one of the researchers at that time:

"We set up a telephone connection between us and the guys at SRI," Kleinrock in LA said in an interview.

"We typed the L and we asked on the phone, 'Do you see the L?'

"'Yes, we see the L,' came the response.

"We typed the O, and we asked, 'Do you see the O?'

"'Yes, we see the O.'

"Then we typed the G, and the system crashed ... Yet a revolution had begun."[14]

In 1981, the US National Science Foundation created the computer science network expanding access to the ARPANET; and in 1986 "provided access to supercomputer sites for research and education organizations."[15] It was not until 1992 that the final restrictions on

---

[14] Peter Clement, *The State of the Net,* 9.

[15] Wikipedia, History of the Internet.

the commercial use of the internet were removed, and commercial use started to become widespread.[16]

Internet access was originally provided by internet information services, such as CompuServe and America Online (AOL). By 1995, internet access was being obtained directly through Internet Service Providers (ISPs), generally the telephone and cable companies. The cable modem had been developed to allow internet access at faster speeds through the networks of the TV cable companies.[17]

At about this time, the number of computers connected to the internet began to take off in earnest. In 1994, about 3 million computers were connected to the internet; in 1995, the number reached about 6.6 million; and by 1997, the number exceeded 16 million. Thereafter, the number of connected computers grew exponentially.[18]

Internet Standards (Protocols)

The internet as we know it today is not a single network but a network of networks that link individual devices (in our case, personal computers) through local area networks and wide area networks to larger networks linked through routers that pass data from one network to another. The routers are large computers that act as gateways between networks and "process, filter, forward, route and pass packets from one network to another."[19]

To make this communication system work, there must be a universal set of standards governing all the steps required in the network communication process. Fortunately, these were developed and made available free of charge.

The internet standards are set out in layers, in which each layer deals with a separate aspect of the internet communication process. These layers are complex and not easy for nontechnical people to comprehend.

---

[16] Gregory Gromov, *Roads and Crossroads of Internet History.*
[17] Peter Clement, *The State of the Net.*
[18] Ibid.
[19] Daniel Minoli, *Internet and Internet Engineering*, 38.

The most general set of standards for networking are set out in the seven-layer Open Systems Interconnection Reference Model developed by the International Organization for Standardization (ISO) to establish protocols to allow communication over networks connecting computers and other devices, regardless of the hardware and software used to establish the network. (See Appendix E for a fuller description of the hierarchy of network standards.)

Perhaps the most important set of internet standards is referred to as the TCP/ IP protocols (Transport Control Protocols and Internet Protocols). These were first developed in 1982 to provide standardized routing and communications of data across an interconnected network of computers.[20] They are the main set of protocols used on the internet to this day. (See Appendix E, A Hierarchy of Network Standards).

For the most part, these network protocols are embedded in the personal computer's operating system and Web browser software.

Another set of protocols that is essential to the universal operation of the internet governs the formatting of data to be transmitted over the internet.

These were developed in 1989 by Tim Berners-Lee "when he conceived the idea for a global hypertext system that would facilitate the sharing of information … around the world."[21]

Berners-Lee's hypertext system consisted of three protocols:

(1) The Hypertext Transmission Protocol (HTTP), allowing Web browsers to communicate with Web servers,
(2) The Hypertext Markup Language (HTML), the language in which web pages are written, and
(3) Uniform Resource Locators (URLs), which provide the addresses used to identify web pages and other information on the internet.

---

[20] Clement, *The State of the Net*, 10.
[21] Behrouz Forouzan, *Data Communications and Networks* (1990), 525.

The last piece of the internet standard's puzzle was developed in the early 1990s by Marc Andreessen. It came to be the Web browser: "a final piece of software, resident on the user's computer, through which the elements of HTML code could be viewed."[22]

All these standards came together, free of charge, to form the public data communications media, the internet.

At about the same time, say 1995, this new communications facility set off the building of the physical networks that would carry information around the world. A group of companies, including Nortel from Canada and Global Crossing, as well as the telephone and cable companies, started laying fiber optic cables within cities, across countries, and beneath the oceans. A little later, companies began launching communication satellites to enable people with computers in remote areas not serviced by cable to access the internet wirelessly. The use of the internet exploded after 1995 and with it the sales of personal computers.

---

[22] Clement, *The State of the Net,* 12.

PC Sales, 1996 to 2012[23]

Year	Sales in Million $
1996	70
1997	80
1998	92
1999	113
2000	134
2001	128
2002	132
2003	168
2004	189
2005	218
2006	239
2007	271
2008	302
2009	305
2010	351
2011	352
2012	352

We can see from this table from Wikipedia, obtained from surveys carried out annually by the Gartner Group, that PC sales grew rapidly from 1996 to 2012. The coincident arrival of the commercial and open internet in the 1990s, and within this service, the ability to communicate by email, was a major contributor to the spectacular growth in PC sales in this period.

---

[23] PC sales include sales of Desktop, laptop and workstation computers but not iPads and similar notebooks.

Email

While people found many uses for the internet over the following years, the predominant use has been email. "Since the mid 1990s, the Internet has had a revolutionary impact on culture and commerce, including the rise of near instant communication by electronic mail, instant messaging, Voice over Internet 'phone calls' and many other uses."[24] This is still true today (2021). (See this quote from a 2012 publication, *Complete iPad for Seniors*: "The ability to stay in touch via Email from anywhere in the world is one of the main reasons to own an iPAD.")

In the last half of the 1990s, the ubiquity, speed, and convenience of communicating by email led to large increases in annual sales of personal computers, the primary device for connecting to the internet at that time.

Email is enabled by a software program embedded in a personal computer's Web browser. The software sends an email to servers that accept, store, and forward the messages to the intended recipients.

Each email message has three components: an envelope, a message, and a header that contains the sender's email address, the recipient's email address, and information about the message such as the date, subject, and the message itself. The envelope provides communication information using the Simple Mail Transfer Protocol (SMTP) to enable the internet to route the email from its sender to the intended recipients.

---

[24] Wikipedia, History of the Internet.

Once the email has been forwarded and stored in a server, software adhering to either the POP or IMAP protocols allowed the ultimate recipient to retrieve the email on a personal communication device, which in the 1990s was a personal computer. (See also Appendix E.)

Email greatly raised the bar for speed of communications and the ability to communicate simultaneously with multiple recipients. The general result was a huge increase in convenience and, most importantly, a huge reduction in cycle times throughout a business and in communications with customers and suppliers. This in turn enabled significant savings in our big three factors: time, quality, and costs, with matching advances in competitive positioning.

Dell Revisited

Now let us look at what the internet did to Dell Computers' business. As we saw above, Dell's business methodology, integrated manufacturing, was highly dependent on good communications, within the company and with Dell's select group of suppliers. The arrival of the internet and email gave a real boost to the integrated manufacturing methodology. It sped up and simplified the communications required by the methodology. This in turn served to increase the competitive advantage provided by it. As we can see from the previous table, PC sales doubled over five years, from 1995 to 2000. Dell, with its direct sales-based methodology and integrated manufacturing management system, was a leading participant in these sales increases and in 2001 became the global leader in PC sales, surpassing Compaq, which had been the leader for several years. While Hewlett-Packard took over the lead in 2001, after it acquired Compaq, this was a one-year phenomenon. Dell regained the lead in 2002 and held it through 2006.

Text Messaging

Text messaging actually predates the internet and email. The origin of text messaging can be traced to the Short Message Service (SMS). The first SMS message was sent in December 1992, when Neil Papworth, a test engineer for the SEMA Group, used a PC to send "Merry Christmas" as a message to the phone of colleague Richard Jarvis. SMS soon became available to all cellular networks and was a widely used communication system (and still is today). "By the end of 2010, SMS was the most widely used data application, with an estimated 3.5 billion active users," who sent over 6 trillion messages in that year.

The SMS service was developed for mobile phone users to send messages to each other over the phone network systems. This is still likely the most common use today, although with the arrival of the internet in 1995, the service has been expanded to included messages over the internet. Today, the SMS system is imbedded in smartphone and PC operating systems.[25]

One of the attractive features of text messaging is that the system tells users when the message has been delivered and, even more importantly, when it has been read. Hence the achievement of instant messaging. Other enhancements include the ability to send photos and videos in the message, as well as emojis to express feelings.

---

[25] Wikipedia, Text Messaging.

Instant messaging systems over the internet have also grown since 1995. WhatsApp, first released in 2009, is one of these systems. WhatsApp was acquired by Facebook in 2014. It has the advantage of avoiding international telephone charges. Wikipedia reports that "it became the most popular messaging App by 2015 and had more than 2 billion users worldwide by February 2020."[26]

---

[26] Wikipedia, WhatsApp.

Three Headwinds

In the first decade of the twenty-first century, the PC industry found itself fighting three separate headwinds.

(1) The first of these occurred in 2000 and 2001; the bursting of the dot.com bubble that eventually took down the whole technology industry and slowed the growth in PC sales.
(2) The second headwind was the financial crisis of 2008 that slowed down all economic activity for an extended period.
(3) The third headwind, and the most important for the PC, was the arrival of the smartphone and later the iPad. The smartphone started to take off in 2004 when Research In Motion (RIM) launched its BlackBerry.

Mike Lazaridis, Jim Balsillie and the BlackBerry[27]

When Mike Lazaridis was a teenager, he established himself as the Go-to-guy for fixing broken computers and other electronic devices. He attended Waterloo University where he studied electrical engineering and computer science. While a student, Lazaridis and fellow students built a computer-like device that allowed users to type words and see them flashed on a TV screen. In their fourth year at Waterloo, they

---

[27] Wikipedia: Mike Lazaridis.

decided to launch a business by selling the device to other businesses. On March 7, 1984, they created a new company, calling it Research In Motion Ltd.[28]

The Business did not initially prosper, and the boys made ends meet by making various electronic components for companies like GM. Fortunately they met Ted Rogers, the Canadian cable TV baron, and he hired them to investigate a purchase of components for a wireless data network called Mobitex, with which they became very familiar.

Years passed, but in 1992, when RIM was still struggling, Jim Balsillie was introduced to Mike Lazaridis. Balsillie had completed an education course that included graduating from Trinity College at the University of Toronto. His next step was to join the accounting firm of Clarkson Gordon (now Ernst & Young) in Toronto. In that firm he joined a group that I happened to be heading up called the Venture Group; It had been formed to target entrepreneurs building young, innovative companies, with our services that included, in addition to the traditional accounting and auditing services, advice on strategic planning and financing. After obtaining his CPA degree, Balsillie left Clarkson Gordon to attend Harvard University where he earned his MBA.

Returning to Waterloo, Canada, Balsillie made some money straightening out another Waterloo based technology company. Over time, Balsillie and Lazaridis negotiated a deal in which Balsillie would invest a much-needed cash injection of $125,000 for 30 percent of RIM and they agreed to a unique leadership arrangement where they would be co-CEOs of the company.

In 1996, after several years of selling modems for Mobitex use, Lazaridis conceived the idea of creating a mobile message device that would be a simple-to-use, and inexpensive, handheld device that could send and receive messages quickly. After several false starts, RIM came up with a small two-way pager, nicknamed the Leapfrog, that used email to transmit data. It allowed a user to input data using two thumbs on a keyboard. As things turned out this two thumbs input became addictive.

---

[28] The BlackBerry story was extracted from Jacquie McNish and Sean Silcoff, *Losing the Signal* (2016).

Later still, the handheld two-way email device was renamed the BlackBerry.

How did they come up with this unusual name? Many of RIM's engineers liked the name PocketLink. Other choices included EasyMail and MegaMail. But marketing vice president, Dave Werezak felt these names were anxiety triggers. What was needed was a name that lowered workers' blood pressure. Staff considered soothing and positive names such as "melon" and "strawberry." These too were rejected. One of the employees suggested "blackberry." A linguistics professor pointed out that the letter B "was a positive sound evoking speed and efficiency." When Lazaridis heard this suggestion, he liked it immediately, and the decision was made to use the name blackberry, but to emphasize the bs by capitalizing them to form "BlackBerry."[29]

Balsillie decided to take advantage of the addictiveness of the BlackBerry by offering it to senior bankers and lawyers and through them to the senior executives of Fortune 1000 companies. Once these leaders had BlackBerrys, they insisted their staff get them too. Sales took off.

The RIM stock was listed on the Nasdaq Index and when sales took off, so did the stock, hitting $156 in March 2000, valuing RIM at about $11 billion.

A special feature of the BlackBerry from the start was its security. BlackBerry emails were encrypted on sending and decrypted on receipt by coding that was unique to each customer. This was especially attractive to business executives and became an important selling feature.

In 2004, RIM added a speaker and a microphone to the BlackBerry, and the smartphone was born.

---

[29] McNish and Silcoff, *Losing the Signal.*

Through this period, sales of BlackBerrys were buoyant, as set out in the following table:

BlackBerry Sales, Income, and Market Cap, in $

Year	Sales	Income	Market Cap in December
2005	1.350 billion	206 million	12.15 billion
2006	2.066 billion	375 million	24 billion
2007	3.037 billion	637 million	59 billion
2008	6.009 billion	1294 million	23 billion
2009	11.065 billion	1893 million	39 billion
2010	14.953 billion	2457 million	32 billion
2011	19.907 billion	3411 million	7 billion
2012	18.423 billion	1164 million	6 billion
2013	11.073 billion	-646 million	3.8 billion
2014	6.813 billion	-5873 million	5.75 billion
2015	3.335 billion	-304 million	4.53 billion
2016	2.160 billion	-208 million	3.69 billion
2017	1.309 billion	-1206 million	6.18 billion
2018	0.932 billion	405 million	3.73 billion
2019	0.904 billion	93 million	3.57 billion
2020	1.040 billion	-152 million	5.72 billion
2021	0.893 billion	-1104 million	5.02 billion

From this chart [30], we can see that BlackBerry sales continued to climb reaching a peak in 2011 of $19.907 billion. Net income also climbed to a peak of $3.411 billion in 2011. From 2012 to 2021 sales dropped dramatically, while net income bounced around but generally fell in this period. Market cap peaked in 2007 at $59 billion and fell thereafter, suggesting investors anticipated a decline to come in BlackBerry's business.

What are the events that lie behind these statistics?

---

[30] Macrotrends on BlackBerry.

After introducing the smartphone to the public in 2004, life should have been rosy. But in the next three years, BlackBerry suffered three calamitous setbacks.

The first was a patent dispute initiated by a US patent troller, NTP. It accused Blackberry of breaching patents it had acquired and took it to court. The dispute started in 2001 and lasted five years. BlackBerry finally settled it with a payment of $612 million in March of 2006. This dispute took a large amount of BlackBerry management time and was devastating to the morale of the two co-CEOs.

The second crisis arose around the backdating of stock options. This was a common practice of technology companies and others at this time. In a volatile stock market, it was often necessary to backdate options to ensure they would be meaningful incentives to employees. The practice was not illegal, provided it was properly reported to shareholders. BlackBerry and other companies, including Apple, failed to meet security commission requirements for this reporting. While the dispute with the security commission went on for several years, it was finally settled in 2008 with penalty payments of about $90 million. It was "one of the largest set of sanctions ever paid by officers of a Canadian company." As bad as the penalties were, it was the effect the dispute had on the relationship of the co-CEOs that badly hurt BlackBerry. They never worked as well together after this time.

The third crisis for the BlackBerry company was caused by Steve Jobs. In 2007, Jobs announced the arrival of the Apple iPhone. He did this in true Mike Markkula fashion (if you are introducing an innovative product, you should do it in an innovative way). Jobs introduced the iPhone at an assembly of four thousand journalists and cheering employees. The iPhone, he explained, was a handheld device that combined both digital and telephone communication facilities. To increase the appeal to consumers, the iPhone had a camera and could play and record music. And taking dead aim at BlackBerry, he explained that the "awkward keyboard" would be replaced by a touchscreen keyboard that was more intuitive and easier to operate.

While BlackBerry made several efforts to match the iPhone, none were successful. In spite of these crises, BlackBerry smartphones continued to sell very well until about 2011, when they hit a high of annual sales of $19.907 billion and a net income of $3,411 million. After this point, sales fell off quite dramatically and after 2012, net income disappeared.

Management and engineering problems continued to manifest themselves at BlackBerry, and after considerable pressure from disgruntled shareholders, in January of 2012, the two CEOs decided to resign their titles. Shortly thereafter, Balsillie left the company for good, and Lazaridis followed the next year.

Eventually, the BlackBerry smartphone was discontinued, and the company shifted strategy to building a software business based on the modular operating system developed by QNS, an Ottawa, Canada-based company which BlackBerry had acquired. In due course, John Chen was brought in from Silicon Valley to steer this change in direction. The QNX microkernel operating system was tailor made for the electronic operation and communication required for the Internet of Things (IOT). The security features of the system were also important to the IOT where security concerns were limiting the applications of the system. The QNX system has been very popular for the electronic systems in today's automotive industry. BlackBerry estimates that its QNX system can be found in more than 195 million vehicles. So, the company is still going.

Despite the unhappy demise of the BlackBerry smartphone and the resulting troubles of the company, BlackBerry has left many wonderful legacies to Waterloo and to Canada. It established Waterloo and Waterloo University as an important technology research center, strengthening Waterloo University's co-op program as an important source of technology research and development students. Mike Lazaridis established two research foundations: the Perimeter Institute for Theoretical Physics and the Institute for Quantum Computing, two leading-edge research vehicles. Balsillie established the Balsillie School of International Affairs, a center for research on global governance and international public policy, and has acted as an advisor to many technology entrepreneurs. And of course, BlackBerry's success made many employees and shareholders rich beyond their dreams. A great Canadian business story.

Three Tailwinds

In the first decade of the twenty-first century, PC sales continued to rise, reaching 218 million units in 2005 and 308 million units in 2009.[31] This continued growth coincided with (1) the development of the World Wide Web as a universal source of information, (2) the use of the internet as a sales channel, and (3) the advent of a new phenomenon, social media.

---

[31] Wikipedia, Personal Computer/sales.

The World Wide Web

The development of the WWW as an information source, providing information from around the world to a connected device anywhere, occurred much more slowly than the take up of email outlined above, even though both started to be available commercially at about the same time in the 1990s. Undoubtedly, this slower development can be attributed to the time taken for people to create the websites and populate them with useful information. For example, Wikipedia, the internet's free encyclopedia, was started in 2001, and its first articles were written late in 2001 and 2002. "As of October 2021 [, it] has the most articles of any edition, at 6,468,441."[32]

The World Wide Web can be distinguished from the internet. "The WWW connects computers that provide information (servers) with computers that ask for it (clients), the communication devices used by individuals like you and me. The Web uses the Internet to make the connection and carry the information."[33] (See a video clip describing how the internet works.) [34]The use of the WWW as an information source required the creation of better and better web browsers.

---

[32] Wikipedia.org/wiki/English Wikipedia.
[33] Brian Kernighan, *D Is for Digital*, chapter 10, "The World Wide Web."
[34] http://wimp.com/internet works/How-the-internet-works.

The Web Browser

The web browser is an application software program residing in the operating system of a computer that is designed to go out into the internet to obtain information from a URL web location known to the user and bring it back to the user's PC.

The first commercially popular Web browser was developed by Mark Andreessen in 1994. Andreessen used the Web browser to create his company, Netscape, and called the Web browser the Netscape Navigator. For years, it was the dominant browser, until Microsoft developed the Internet Explorer browser and effectively used its monopoly of Windows in PC operating systems to squeeze out Netscape's Navigator. In due course, Internet Explorer (now Microsoft Edge) became the dominant browser. In the 2000s, Internet Explorer's dominant position was challenged by competitive browsers, include Mozilla's Firefox, Google's Chrome, Safari for Apple, and Opera.

Search Engines

From these descriptions, we can see that the creation of efficient and reliable WWW search engines is an integral part of using the internet. A search engine is a particular website through which users can search through internet websites.

A search engine has three main components.

(1) A web crawler, which is a software program that regularly scans websites automatically for URLs, key words, and links in order to discover the sought-after information.

(2) An index of URLs, links, and keywords found by the crawler.

(3) A search algorithm, which searches the index and matches the results to key words inserted by the user.

A search engine maintains its own database of URLs, links, and keywords.

Sergei Brin, Larry Page and Google

Google, the creator of the most popular search engine, was founded in 1998, went public in 2004, and had a market capitalization of $200 billion in 2010 and $1.9 trillion in 2021.[35]

Google was founded by Sergey Brin and Larry Page, who were both students at Stanford University, doing PhDs in computer science. After they met in 1995, they got along and quickly became the best of friends. Both were sons of university professors and "had a healthy disregard for the impossible."[36]

Page's father, Carl Page, was a professor of computer science at the University of Michigan. His mother was a database consultant with a master's degree in computer science. So Page was quite familiar with computers and an early user of the personal computer.

Brin's father, Michael, was a math professor at the University of Maryland, and his mother was a scientist at NASA's Goddard Space Flight Center. Thus, Brin was also well acquainted with computers and their operation. "Every member of the Brin family had a home page on the Internet that was linked to one another." After graduating from Maryland, Brin went to Stanford University, where in due course he met Page.

---

[35] David A. Vise and Mark Malseed, *The Google Story.*

[36] Wikipedia: Google.

One night, Page had the crazy idea that he was going to download the entire web to his computer. There was no thought of making it available to others, let alone the thought of building a business.

In pursuit of his idea, Page began to explore the newly created Web. Brin was interested in data mining and making sense of the information, and so he began to help Page fulfill his dream.

Alta Vista was the primary search engine at this time. It was good in looking around the internet but was weak in ranking the search results. The Alta Vista search results included the location of links. Links (now called hyperlinks) allowed computer users to click on a highlighted word or words to be taken to another website with more information about the words clicked.

Page decided to focus on the links. He theorized that counting the number of links to a particular website could be used to rank its popularity and importance.

Brin and Page began to work on the development of a new search engine and came up with a system to count the number of links to a website discovered in a search as a way to rank the popularity of the websites reached in the search.

Based on this system of ranking popularity, they were able to develop a new search system that returned prioritized results based on relevance. This was a huge advantage over Alta Vista.

An interesting aspect of the Google story is that they offered searches to users for free. The key to Google's profitability is advertising. By tracking the user's search results, Google obtained powerful data for advertising. Advertisers have flocked to advertise on Google's search results ever since.

A key to the success of Google becoming a highly profitable business is Eric Schmidt.

Eric Schmidt was introduced to Brin and Page by the eminent venture capitalist John Doerr, who was an investor in Google. After some serious discussions Schmidt was signed on as the chairman of the board and quickly thereafter as the CEO of Google. As CEO, he looked after the management of the business, leaving Brin and Page free to pursue their dreams of building the best search engine in the world.

Schmidt was eminently qualified for the job. He was an electrical engineering grad of Princeton University and earned a PhD in electrical engineering from the University of California. He worked at Bell Labs, Zilog, and Xerox Palo Alto Research Center (PARC) before joining Sun Microsystems as a software manager, going on to become the chief technology officer.

In 1997, Schmidt left Sun Microsystems and joined Novell as CEO and chairman of the board.

Novell

Novell was one of the early personal computer software stars. It was founded in 1980 by George Canova and Jack Davis, in Orem, Utah, and went public in 1985. Its CEO during much of its prime period was Ray Noorda. Under his leadership, Novell's NetWare became the dominant personal computing networking software, long before the arrival of the public internet. Its primary product, NetWare, was the backbone of local area networks (LANs) and enabled PC users to communicate and collaborate with fellow users without tying up the time on mainframes. By the early 1990s, there were over half a million such LANs using NetWare with more than 50 million users. In 1994, its revenue peaked at $2 billion.

However, Novell was up against Microsoft. When the PC software giant included networking services in its PC operating system Windows NT, it gradually displaced NetWare as the LAN of choice. Schmidt was involved in trying to enable Novell to fend off the overwhelming competition from Microsoft, competition that eventually ended Novell's life in 2014. It was an experience that would stand him in good stead at Google.

In order to build the best search engine, Page and Brin focussed on investing in two areas: hardware and software. On the hardware side, they built a large and growing network of personal computers, modified by them to hold the growing index of websites for the search engine. At the same time, they saw that continuous innovation in search would require hiring many top-notch software engineers. They invested heavily in recruiting software researchers. This was a special area where Schmidt made a huge contribution.

As their search business grew, "encompassing virtually the entire known Web and surpassing anything anyone else had done,"[37] they were creating serious competition for Microsoft by threatening its domination of PC software. The battle was in full force. And a large part of the battle was the recruiting of the best and brightest software engineers. Schmidt decided to get involved.

In May of 2005, Schmidt embarked on a recruiting mission in Microsoft's home territory in Seattle. He gave a lecture to a large group of computer science students at the University of Washington to persuade them that getting a software research position at Google would be far better than going to Microsoft. He made these points:

(1) He described Microsoft as an "aging giant whose best days were behind it."[38] "Microsoft," he said, "was rooted in an earlier phase of technology that had been surpassed by the power of the Internet revolution."

(2) Google researchers were organized in small teams of three to five persons, each "working on high visibility, high impact projects" of their choosing.

(3) "Our rate of innovation is significantly faster than anyone in the industry."

(4) When asked about the supervision of researchers, he stated that Google liked to have "as little middle management as possible."[39]

All these points were music to the ears of the research students. They were a perfect fit with Google's twofold approach to building the best

---

[37] Vise, *The Google Story,* 237.

[38] Ibid., 265.

[39] Quotes are from Vise, *The Google Story.*

search engine ever: (1) lots of computing power through their customized PCs, and (2) hiring the best researchers and treating them well.

In 2021, Google generated revenue for nine months of $182 million, of which $22.8 million went to research, leaving net income of $55 million.

It appears to us that the Google story is just beginning, and more good things lie in its future.

Armed with the search engine tools, anyone can go to the WWW to obtain information on virtually any subject and at incredible levels of detail. In 2013, for example, it was possible to obtain from the WWW information about a medical procedure that rivals the knowledge of the medical profession; the details of the procedure, how to prepare for it, the risks of the procedure, and in many cases, the success rate of it: all very helpful in deciding whether to go ahead with the procedure or not.

E-commerce

The next internet growth driver in the 2000s was the development of e-commerce, the use of the internet as a sales channel. This use of the internet developed even more slowly than the use of the WWW to access information, and with good reason. Most retailers were very leery about using the internet for sales of products and services because they were afraid of upsetting their existing channels and relationships. So, for example, a large retail chain with many existing retail stores did not want to create a sales channel that would bypass its existing store and take away sales that would otherwise have gone to one of them. There were different options for handling this dilemma.

On the one hand, retailers sought to use the internet as a means of supporting their existing stores. For example, they used the internet to provide prospective customers with the locations of their stores, with the goods for sale in those stores, and more recently, with the specific number of each item in any particular store.

Other retailers sought to use the internet as a sales channel for goods that could be distributed more easily from central warehouses rather than through existing stores and sought to avoid the conflicting internal interests in this way. Some, such as Walmart, did both.

| Jeff Bezos and Amazon

And then along came Amazon. Amazon didn't have these conflicts because it didn't have any retail stores. Amazon was incorporated in 1994 and first went online in 1995. Initially, it used the internet as a sales channel to sell books, and it set up an elaborate supporting infrastructure of warehouses, publisher relationships, and book catalogues to fulfill the sales orders. Later, as we will write, it realized the full potential of e-commerce by providing customers with a device, the Kindle book reader, on which to download their book orders electronically. This crucial step eliminated much of the hassle of traditional retailing both for its customers and for itself. Let's look at the story of how Amazon was created and developed. *Time* magazine made Amazon founder Jeff Bezos its 1999 Person of the Year. Here is how they tell the story:

In 1994, Bezos, a Princeton graduate in electrical engineering and computer science (reminiscent of Steve Wozniak), was employed by D.E. Shaw, "an unusual firm that prided itself on hiring some of the smartest people in the world and then figuring out what kind of work they might profitably do."

Bezos's job with Shaw was to research new business opportunities. In this capacity, he became intrigued by the young communications media, the internet, and set about trying to determine "what kind of business opportunity might there be here?" Through the facilities at Shaw, Bezos could see that the use of the internet was expanding in leaps and bounds, and he was drawn to the opportunities it was creating for e-commerce. He was looking for a way to use the internet to create "the most [unique] value for customers." "Value" to Bezos would be something customers craved: selection, convenience, and low prices, value that would make it compelling for them to switch to a brand-new way of buying.

In due course, he settled on books. After doing some serious research, Bezos discovered that book wholesalers had their catalogues digitized, on CD ROMs that would be relatively easy to put online.

Bezos opened the virtual doors of Amazon.com's online store in July 1995, and the company, an instant success, grew like topsy. But it wasn't until the release of the Amazon e-book reader, the Kindle, in 2007 that Amazon.com realized its full potential in e-commerce, introducing a large improvement in convenience and price for its customers and greatly simplifying its own business model. I had bought a few books from Amazon.com prior to the introduction of the Kindle, because of the huge catalogue of books it had. ("In 2011, it had a stated library of over 850,000 titles.") But I was an early purchaser of the Kindle and became amazed at how easy it was to buy a book using the Kindle (perhaps too easy), and how quickly the Whispernet system downloaded the book to the Kindle (and later to other devices and platforms, such as tablet computers).

Amazon.com has added many features to the e-book sales and download system, including reviews, the ability to download a sample of a book, better displays, choice of font size, the ability to add footnotes, as well as ease of payment features. About the only thing you can't do easily is loan your favorite book to a friend.

However, the world of e-commerce and e-books has become much more competitive since Amazon obtained the "First Mover" advantage. For example, both Barnes & Noble in the United States and Indigo in Canada have come out with their own e-book readers, the NOOK, and the KOBO, respectively, and now achieve a significant portion of their sales on these devices.

Other competitors such as eBay have used the internet to create a "many-to-many" approach to selling and have been very successful in so doing. In response, Amazon.com has added a whole new array of products, from luxury goods to doggie pee pads. It acts as a sales channel for other vendors and has also developed a program, CreateSpace, for authors to self-publish their literary efforts through Amazon.com.

Amazon.com has been a stock market success from its IPO in 1997 and has continued to do well for its shareholders throughout the twenty-first century, despite a few hiccups such as the bursting of the dot.com bubble in 2000. It continues to have a huge impact on retailing of all kinds. In 2013, "the shutting of eight Future shops and seven Best Buy big box stores across the country [Canada] comes as electronics retailers feel the squeeze of the burgeoning business of online retailers." The cuts follow a similar move in March 2012, in the United States, where the parent company said it was closing fifty stores. [40]

---

[40] *Toronto Globe and Mail*, "Report on Business" (February 1, 2013).

Social Media

A third driver of internet usage in the 2000s was the arrival of social media. In this book, "social media" refers to the use of the internet and World Wide Web to enable people and groups of people to interact by exchanging information about themselves, including pictures and videos, about topics that interest them, and about links to websites of interest to them.

This phenomenon has both a positive side and a negative side. On the positive side, it enables an exchange of information at speeds that could only have been dreamed about just a few years ago; the exchange of information by people around the globe and among groups of people with common interests, some of which are discovered through social media themselves. On the negative side, one result is an explosion in the amount of data each of us is exposed to that often leads to information overload and an inability to handle the quantity of information rationally. A second, and perhaps more nefarious, negative, is the impact on our individual, or group, privacy of personal information. We will discuss this aspect further below when we look at Facebook, since it has tried to address some of these privacy concerns.

One of the important features of social media is that it has become highly interactive. This is exemplified by the popularity of blogs and Tweets, as we discuss below. It has facilitated the collaboration of groups of people with common interests at high speeds and from global locations. As such, it is a very innovative tool that encourages unprecedented innovation in its turn. "Social Media differentiates from traditional/industrial media in many aspects, such as quality, reach, frequency, usability, immediacy and permanence."[41]

A variety of software enabled tools to facilitate use of this new media have sprung up in the first decade of the twenty-first century, and more are being developed daily. We will look at a few of the more popular tools to show how the new media is being used. We will look at Facebook, blogging, Twitter, microblogging, LinkedIn, Skype, and YouTube.

The internet usage effects of social media, according to Nielsen, are that internet users continue to spend more time on social media platforms than any other sites. "The total time spent on Social Media in the U.S. across PC and mobile devices increased by 37 percent to 121 billion minutes in July 2012 compared to 88 billion minutes in July 2011."

According to Statista, it is estimated that in 2020, there were around 3.6 billion people using social media around the globe, up from 3.4 billion in 2019. Statista, in January of 2021, lists the three most used social media platforms as Facebook with 2.740 million users, YouTube with 2.291 million users, and WhatsApp with 2 million users.

Mark Zuckerberg and Facebook

Facebook is the leading social media tool in use today. It was launched by Mark Zuckerberg in 2004. [42]

Zuckerberg was a student at Harvard University in 2003.[43] At that time, Harvard had a student directory, called "face book," featuring photos and personal information. It was only available on paper. Zuckerberg decided to create a website version and launched it in January of 2004 with the name "Thefacebook."[44]

---

[41] Wikipedia on Social Media.
[42] Wikipedia, Facebook.
[43] Ben Mezrich, *The Accidental Billionaires.*
[44] Wikipedia: Facebook.

This drew the attention of Tyler and Cameron Winklevoss and Divya Narenda, who claimed that Zuckerberg had stolen their ideas. Later, they sued Zuckerberg and eventually won a settlement of about $170 million.

In the meantime, Zuckerberg, with help from Eduardo Saverin, made the website available to Harvard students, and within a month, half the undergraduates had registered on the website. Two months later, the website was made available to students at Stanford, Columbia, and Yale. It quickly reached students at most universities in Canada and the United States.

Facebook was incorporated in the summer of 2004 and moved to Palo Alto in Silicon Valley. It continued to grow exponentially and had reached 6 million users by the end of 2005. In 2006, Facebook was made available to everyone aged thirteen or older with a valid email address.

Facebook remained a private company for several years while its business was becoming established. The costs in the initial few months were shared by Zuckerberg and Saverin. Later in 2004, Peter Thiel, an angel investor, put $500,000 into the company for 10.2 percent of its shares. In 2005, a venture capital firm, Accel Partners, invested $12.7 million for 13 percent of the company.

Sheryl Sandberg was hired by Facebook as chief operating officer in March of 2008. She was a really valuable steal from Google, where she had been vice president of global online sales and operations, and so she was very familiar with internet growth stars whose main source of revenue was advertising. Prior to that, she had been the chief of staff of US Secretary of the Treasury Lawrence Summers.[45]

Under Sandberg, Facebook decided that advertising would be its source of revenue. After a few changes to its advertising model, Facebook turned profitable in 2009. In 2011, Facebook generated a profit of about $1 billion on advertising revenue of about $3.7 billion.

In 2007, Microsoft bought a small interest (about 1.6 percent) in the company that put a market value on the firm of about $15 billion. It went public on May 17, 2012, with an initial public offering that valued

---

[45] Wikipedia, Sheryl Sandberg.

the company at $104 billion, although the share price fell back almost immediately.

The Facebook web page provides a number of tools to assist the user. In general, it provides a place to list the user's personal information, including photographs and videos, and links to websites of interest. The user can also set and limit the names of other users who may access the user's data.

More features are being created almost daily.

Facebook faces many of the same positives and negatives as listed above for social media generally. It facilitates the sharing of information and communications among individuals and groups, on the one hand, but it raises serious privacy concerns, on the other. The privacy concerns exist in spite of the steps Facebook has taken to try to address them by, for example, letting users limit the people who have access to their information or profile. Nevertheless, this information is in a virtual public domain, and users have no control over how Facebook will use the information or allow others to use it. Facebook derives its revenue almost entirely from advertising and undoubtedly uses the personal profiles to target advertising.

Other more harmful uses may also be possible.

These days, there is increasing concern about identity theft, in which someone steals your identity information and uses it to withdraw money from your bank or even take out a mortgage on a house, without you knowing it until the creditor approaches you for repayment. Because of this type of concern, a lot of people are reluctant to use Facebook and similar social media. On the other hand, many are unconcerned about this or are ignorant of the risks; Facebook is reported to have over 1 billion users, for whom the benefits must outweigh the disadvantages.[46]

---

[46] Wikipedia on Social Media.

Blogging

Blogging refers to software that allows a particular type of publishing on a website. Typically, the author starts a publishing chain by setting up a blog and inviting others to view the Web page, add comments to it, or link to it. Authors can add new material as desired to update the blog and keep it current. It is thus a means of promoting your own material or interests and seeking collaborative participation by others. The original authors may control the participation of others or not. The subject matter is limited only by the author's imagination and can be as ephemeral as, What will the internet look like in ten years? Or as down to earth as, Spys are the best apples, aren't they?

The original facility for creating blogs was Blogger, a web page publishing software program created by Pyra Labs in 1999. The company was bought by Google in 2003 and is hosted on Google's website as a sub domain of blogspot.com. Google has since added many features to enhance the original software and make the task of creating and running a blog easier and more interesting. There are literally millions of blogs enabling the authors to have a voice on the web and engage with others.[47]

Twitter and Microblogging

Microblogging is a type of blog that limits its registered authors and registered visitors to posting text-based messages, called tweets, of at most 140 characters, to a website. Nonregistered visitors can view the chain of tweets but cannot post to it. Microblogging is used primarily for near-instantaneous communications, often to discuss current events. It is most popular among smartphone users but is also available to personal computer users.

Twitter is the name of the website offering the software service to facilitate microblogging tweets. It was created by Jack Dorsey in 2006. He sent his first tweet in that year, and in 2009, a NASA astronaut

---

[47] Google on Blogger.

sent the first tweet from space while on the Space Shuttle Atlantis. The service grew rapidly. In 2007, 1.6 million tweets were posted. As of 2012, there were over 500 million registered users globally, posting over 340 million tweets a day.

Twitter was reported to be the third highest ranked social networking site in January 2009.[48] In 2012, investment management firm BlackRock purchased $80 million of stock from employees, giving the company an implied market value of $9 billion. Twitter went public on the New York Stock Exchange in 2013.

eMarketer, a research firm, estimates that Twitter had advertising revenue of $545 million in 2018, and Wikipedia reported it had a market cap of $25.6 billion in October of that year.

Twitter's financial statements for 2020 showed revenue of $3.72 billion. In the same statements, Twitter reports "monetizable daily active usage" of 192 million in December 2020. An analysis by Pear Analytics for the same period is broken down to show 40.1 percent of tweets are "pointless babble," 37.6 percent are "conversational," and 8.7 percent has "pass-along value."[49]

Tweets are obviously very popular with users. However, they are a vehicle for spreading misinformation and hate language, in spite of Twitter's attempts to limit this type of usage.

LinkedIn

LinkedIn is a website that allows a network of professionals to describe their business to other professionals. It claims to be the "world's largest professional network with millions of members and growing rapidly."

By joining LinkedIn and recording your professional profile on its website, you can control one of the top search results for your name and

> Build and maintain a broader network of professionals
> you can trust.

---

[48] Wikipedia on Twitter.
[49] Ibid.

Find and reconnect with colleagues and classmates. Learn about other companies.

Leverage powerful tools to find and reach the people you need.

Tap into the knowledge of your network. Discover new opportunities.[50]

LinkedIn was founded in 2003 by Reid Hoffman and went public in 2011.

In January 2013, LinkedIn "crossed an important and exciting milestone for the company. LinkedIn now counts over 200 million members as part of our network, with representation in more than 200 countries and territories. We serve our members in 19 different languages around the world."[51]

Since December 2016, LinkedIn has been a wholly owned subsidiary of Microsoft.

As of September 2021, LinkedIn has more than 774 million registered members from over two hundred countries and territories.[52]

Skype

Skype is a software application using proprietary Voice over Internet Protocol (VoIP). It allows registered users to communicate from a computer with other registered users by voice, video, or text messaging. Its main attraction is that Skype-to-Skype calls from computer-to-computer travel over the internet and are free of telephone or long-distance charges.

Skype calls to regular phones or mobile devices bear a small fee.

---

[50] LinkedIn Website.
[51] Ibid.
[52] Wikipedia on LinkedIn.

Skype software was developed in 2003 by Estonians Ahti Heinla, Priit Kasesalu, and Jaan Tallinn. Skype was acquired by Microsoft in 2011 for $8.5 billion.

"On 19 July 2012, Microsoft announced that Skype users have logged 115 billion minutes of calls over the quarter, up 50% since the last quarter."[53]

As of March 2020, Skype was used by 100 million people at least once a month and by 40 million people each day. During the COVID-19 pandemic, Skype lost a large part of its market share to Zoom.

YouTube

"Founded in February 2005, the YouTube software allows billions of people to discover, watch and share originally created videos. YouTube provides a forum for people to connect, inform, and inspire others across the globe."[54]

YouTube was founded by Steve Chen, Chad Hurley, and Jawed Karim. It is headquartered in San Bruno, California.

In October 2006, You Tube was bought by Google for $1.65 billion. Google has changed YouTube's business model so that it no longer generates revenue from advertising alone. YouTube now offers paid content such as movies, network television, and a wide variety of other videos.

In October of 2009, YouTube announced it had more than 1 billion views per day.[55]

YouTube has had an unprecedented social impact, influencing popular culture, and internet trends. In December 2021, YouTube was ranked as the second most visited website in the United States at 4.11 billion visits, behind only Google with 15.63 billion visits, and ahead of Facebook with 3.36 billion visits and Amazon with 2.69 billion visits.[56]

---

[53] Wikipedia on Skype.

[54] YouTube Website.

[55] Ibid.

[56] Semrush.com ranking of top ten most visited Websites.

On the negative side, YouTube has been criticized for facilitating the spreading of misinformation, violations of users' privacy, and other offenses such as facilitating the broadcasting of hate speech. Because of these failings, several countries have blocked access to YouTube.[57]

Other Social Media

There are many other social media facilities on the internet. Together, given their popularity, they constitute an ongoing driver of PC sales. While much social media communications is now accessed by the smartphone and tablet, personal computers are also used. On February 6, 2013, *Information Week* cited Yankee Group analyst Chris Walsh as saying his data suggest that employees still prefer laptops or desktops over tablets for a range of business tasks. It seems this conclusion is also applicable to the use of social media, with the likely exception of Twitter, and accounts for a significant part of the growth in PC sales in the 2000s.

While social media is aimed primarily at building relationships among individuals and groups of like-minded individuals, businesses are increasingly using social media sites as new sales and marketing channels.

As Schroeder and Schroeder Inc., a Toronto consultancy, point out in their white paper on social media, these uses are changing the very nature of business. They argue that "the impact of Social Media is revolutionary; requiring a major change of mindset and approach, in order to keep up with the resulting changes in consumer and business behavior and demands."

Among other things, they point out that people place more trust in the opinions of their friends and independent sources than they do in those of vendors. Social Media is all about building helpful relationships and providing strong sales channels. To effectively use social media, Schroeder says, businesses must retrain their employees and equip them to use it effectively and ensure they provide the right encouragement to their employees to do so.

---

[57] Wikipedia on YouTube.

The Commodity Years

PC global unit sales peaked at 362 million in 2011 and fell off dramatically over the next seven years. At the time, we speculated that the PC may have entered a commodity period in which sales would be determined primarily on price.

One reason for this observation was the entry into the leadership of PC global sales of three Asian PC manufacturers: Lenovo, building on the acquisition of IBM's PC line in 2005; Acer, which acquired Gateway and eMachines in 2007; and Asus. These three companies have benefited from low manufacturing costs, were able to lower the price of personal computers, and joined Dell and Hewlett-Packard in the top five global PC vendors.

While the software developments discussed so far sustained the high growth path of PC sales to 2011, Intel has been leading other chip manufacturers in the evolution of the chips that form the core of the personal computer. As discussed previously, Intel has been able to achieve Moore's law improvements for decades, repeatedly doubling the chip speed, halving the power needed to operate them, and lowering their costs at rates never before experienced in manufacturing (at the exponential rate of halving costs every two years). Similar improvements have been made in the costs of storing data. As a result, the cost of producing PCs has fallen dramatically over the years, in contrast to the costs of practically everything else.

Unfortunately for Dell and other PC manufacturers, the profit margins on personal computers have fallen even faster, making it harder and harder for them to make a profit. This had a deleterious effect on Dell's stock price and more recently Hewlett-Packard, and it undoubtedly contributed to the decline in PC sales after 2011.

Over the next seven years, PC global sales experienced a precipitous decline of about one-third.[58]

We've identified three main causes of the decline:

(1) A slowdown in the PC replacement cycle,
(2) The arrival of the smartphone in 2004 and the tablet computer in 2009, and
(3) The absence of new mega apps.

1. The Slowdown in the PC Replacement Cycle

The serial improvements in the productivity of the PC have not been surrounded by the excitement Apple has generated for the release of each new iPhone. Apple has succeeded in convincing its users that each new model represents a significant improvement on the previous model, such as increased picture clarity, improved feel, better touch and size, and improved multitasking capability, that they must go out and buy the new model. This, by itself, has generated successive waves of increased sales of the iPhone, to Apple's profit and, as the improvements are matched by the other smartphone makers, in a general increase in smartphone sales.

This excitement over new models has not been a feature of PC sales. In part, this may be due to the fact that there is not a clear market leader in PC sales, as Apple is for the smartphone. (Improvements in PC operations have been decidedly less dramatic and more incremental than those of the smartphone.)

Improvements in the speed of the microchip are not being matched by improvements in PC speeds. And it is not clear that greater speed of

---

[58] Statista.

the PC's internal operations is meeting customers' needs. Personally, we find that the speed of our PC has not improved in the recent models, certainly not at the rate of Moore's law. Similarly, while the price of PCs has dropped, this has not occurred at the rate forecast by Moore's law.

Another factor that might have boosted PC sales would be continuous improvements in ease of use and convenience. This seems to have been the case with smartphones but has not been the case with the PC. If anything, the ease of use of the main PC productivity tools, the Excel spreadsheet and Word, have not improved at all. If you don't know your way around the tools, it is not easy to figure them out.

And each new iteration requires a new, often difficult, learning period. The guidance provided in the applications themselves may be useful for computer geeks but are not particularly helpful to the uninitiated user.

Could this disconnection between the measurable improvements in the PC microchips and the operation of the PC itself be attributable to the lack of similar improvements in the PC operating systems? While each release of Windows may have been an improvement on earlier versions, this has not matched the exponential rate of improvements in the microchip, following Moore's law.

2. The Arrival of Smartphones

In 2004, a Canadian company, Research-in-Motion, released the first smartphone, as we have noted. It was a proprietary system with high-level security features that was used for communications by businesses. Because of its proprietary nature, while it met with enough success to allow Research-in-Motion to be very profitable, it was never visualized as a consumer product.

Steve Jobs and the iPhone

In 2007, Apple released the iPhone, which was a consumer product with music management and playing capabilities and with a camera, among other things. The iPhone was an instant hit with consumers and sold like hotcakes, to become a best seller and to propel the smartphone to prominence.

Consumers found it was an ideal communication device because of its size and portability. It had also been made easy to use. The result was the smartphone surpassed the PC in global unit sales. In fact, the smartphone has been outselling the PC by a factor of over 4 to 1, with sales hitting over 1.5 billion annually from 2017 to 2021.

As a result of this success, the smartphone displaced the PC as the primary digital communication and internet access device. This in turn took away from the PC one of its primary uses and undoubtedly has been a major factor in the overall decline in sales of the PC.

At this point, we would like to digress to discuss the experience of Apple after its initial success in introducing the personal computer with the Apple I and Apple II in the 1970s.

The Apple Story

The story of Apple Computer Inc. (now Apple Inc.) started in 1978, when it got the ball rolling on the first, stand-alone personal computer, and today, it is the most valuable public company on earth, at a market capitalization of about $2.9 trillion.[59] It is a story of ups and downs, and shows how Apple conquered the downs and built on the ups over the years.

As we have noted, following the success of the Apple I PC kit, Steve Wozniak and Steve Jobs developed and sold the Apple II, under the business guidance of Mike Markkula. With the introduction of the first PC spreadsheet VisiCalc, the Apple II provided many businesspeople with greatly improved productivity and ease of use, so that sales of the Apple II took off. Apple went public in 1980, with a value of $2 billion.

In the 1980s, Apple was the established leader in the education market. However, in 1981, IBM decided to enter the PC market, using a microprocessor from Intel and an operating system from Microsoft. IBM allowed other manufacturers to clone its PC, and IBM and the clones gradually achieved dominance in the PC sales market (50 percent in 1986 and increasingly thereafter). As a result, Apple's share of the PC market dropped steadily, and in 1996, it was down to 6 percent (per Wikipedia) and continued to drop thereafter, until recently.

---

[59] Walter Isaacson, *Steve Jobs.*

The value of Apple's shares was relatively modest until it began to pick up in 2007. This was in spite of the development of the Macintosh PC, released in 1984, with the first graphic user interface (GUI), a mouse, and the use of icons, all making the Mac PC easier to use than competing products. Unfortunately for Apple, these improvements had not been patented and were replicated by Microsoft for the IBM and IBM clone machines. This eliminated the competitive advantage fairly quickly, so that sales of the Macintosh did not meet Apple's expectations. One consequence of this failure was that Steve Jobs was fired and replaced as CEO by John Sculley. At about the same time, Steve Wozniak retired to become a teacher.

Under Sculley, Apple steadily improved the Mac. But the real boost came from Apple's introduction in 1985 of PageMaker, a publishing app that allowed businesses to produce professional-looking documents more cheaply and conveniently than before. The graphics arts and publishing businesses quickly became the Mac's most important market. Nevertheless, Apple's share of the PC market continued to erode and with it, Apple's share price.

After a series of other hiccups that drove Apple to the brink of bankruptcy, Steve Jobs was rehired in 1985. He was placed in control and gradually undertook the righting of the company, by focussing it on its main markets of publishing and education. In 1998, Apple launched the iMac with a lower price; it sold very well and lifted Apple back to profitability.

In 2007, Apple introduced the iPhone. Steve Jobs did it with the flare suggested by Mike Markkula's marketing mantra, "if you are announcing an innovative new product, do it in an innovative way." The announcement was made on January 7, 2007, at a San Francisco conference center packed with "tech reporters, bloggers, and cheering employees" (from *Losing the Signal: The Story of the Rise and Fall of BlackBerry*).

The iPhone was a smartphone aimed at the consumer market, which was not BlackBerry's target market when it launched its device in 2004, aimed at businesses wanting to improve their communication capabilities.

Jobs saw that individuals would find the smartphone as useful a device for communications as businesspeople. To increase its attractiveness to consumers, Jobs combined the telephone with the email communication facilities of the smartphone and added a camera and iPod's music-playing capabilities. He also highlighted the simplification of the typing input replacing the button keyboard with keys right on the iPhone's screen.

Demand for the iPhone was high from the start. Roughly one million were purchased in the first few days after its release.

At about the same time, Apple introduced a chain of stores where iPhones could be purchased along with peripheral accessories such as cases, hearing attachments, and a huge array of apps for iPhones, iPads, and iMacs.

In 2010, Apple introduced the iPad, with touchscreen operations like the iPhone. It was a device that in size was between the iPhone and laptop computers. It also sold very well, helping Apple's return to profitability.

In 2011, Apple launched the iCloud, a computer storage service. The iCloud stored the user's applications and data such as photographs, calendars, and music; data could be transferred to the user's other Apple devices via the iCloud.

In 2011, Apple also introduced Siri, a voice-activated personal assistant that could respond to verbal instructions, search the Web for information, and speak the results.

2011 was also the year Tim Cook became the CEO of Apple, succeeding Steve Jobs, who unfortunately succumbed to cancer.

All of the changes in the last few years boosted Apple's profitability and stock market value. In 2018, Apple became the first public company to reach a market value of $1 trillion. And in 2019, it was first to reach $2 trillion. Today, it is the most valuable public company in the world, worth about $2.9 trillion.

It is interesting to consider how Apple has achieved this value, since its share of the PC market has been so low for some years, and even its leading share of the smartphone market is under steady challenge from Samsung and others. We see some clues in the current financial statements.

No one has expressed it better than the CFO. "Our record September quarter [in 2021] results capped off a remarkable fiscal year of strong double-digit growth," said Luca Maestri, Apple's CFO. "The combination of our record sales performance, unmatched customer loyalty, and strength of our ecosystem drove our active installed base of devices to a new all-time high."

Steve Jobs, Tim Cook and the Apple Ecosystem

Looking at the 2021 financials, we can see that iPhone global sales, at $191,973 million, represent more than half of Apple's revenue of $365,817 million. This in spite of the fact that Samsung and other smartphone manufacturers are continually challenging the iPhone's sale leadership. We can see that all sales categories are up in 2021, with services, assumed to include Apple store sales and the sale of a variety of accessories and a plethora of apps for the iPhone, coming in at $68,425 million.

In recent years under Tim Cook, Apple has resurrected its PC sales as well. The iMac has climbed back into the top five in PC sales, Lenovo is in the lead with Hewlett-Packard and Dell vying for second spot, while Apple has been beating out Acer and Asus for fourth spot.

Apple has introduced a new version of the iPhone almost every year since its inception. Each version has significant improvements over the prior model, improvements in simplicity of use, quality of the camera, increased memory capacity, and improved recording quality. And further, Apple has made the switch from one version of the iPhone to the next model straightforward by permitting the automatic transfer of data, icons, and other information. No wonder it has such a loyal base of customers worldwide, a loyal base that is prepared to pay a higher price for Apple products than those of competitors. Its exceptional market value in recent years has been well earned.

3. The Absence of New Mega Apps

It is apparent from the seven-year decline in PC sales volume, from 2011 to 2017, that none of the new apps brought out in this period had the impact on sales that the mega apps, such as the spreadsheet and the word processors, had. Further, none of the recent apps can be considered a mega app. The most recent mega app seems to be the collective apps that constitute social media. This raises the intriguing question: Are more PC software mega apps on the way? We will address this question later in this book.

Very Useful Apps

While there may not have been new mega apps brought out recently, we would be remiss in not mentioning the many smaller apps that are very helpful in particular cases.

Here are two that we have made good use of:

(1) Jacquie Lawson's birthday and other greeting videos. She has a large selection of events from birthdays and anniversaries to Valentine's Day and Christmas for which she has made up very creative and fun videos. You can join her club for twenty dollars a year.

(2) Evite. As the Evite website states, "We make coming together effortless and more memorable for personal and professional events." With Evite's app, you can create your own invitation to weddings, anniversaries, birthday parties, and other events, using a selection of tools to personalize the invitations. Then you can send them as an email. You will receive a notification that your invites have been sent and then a notice of acceptances. The only people you will miss are those who don't use the internet and don't have email addresses (a shrinking group).

There is a plethora of other apps for special purposes. Do you like games?

Gaming software was the main use of the PC in the early days before the spreadsheet and word processing apps were developed. Over the years, gaming apps have shown renewed life. There are many.

We particularly like card game apps, specifically those where you can play bridge online. We use two. The first is Trickster, on which you can come and go as you please. The other is Bridge Base Online, where you can play competitive bridge in games run by your club or open games run by the American Contract Bridge League. Both these card game apps provide random deals, scoring, and other assists. What's more, you may find yourself playing with people from all around the world. If you are on your own, many games allow you to play with robots.

I would also like to mention the Zoom app that allows organizers to set up and run online meetings. Zoom allows video as well as audio participation, perhaps not as sociable as in-person meetings, but very convenient alternatives, and very popular. Zoom is free for low-volume users, a fact that may have encouraged its greater use during the Covid-19 pandemic.

Renewed Growth in PC Sales

We have three more years of global PC sales (2018, 2019, and 2020) to add to our records. From these, we can see that a resurgence in PC sales is happening.

Here are the recent sales volumes:

In 2017, PC sales were 263 million.
In 2018, PC sales were 259 million.
In 2019, PC sales were 261 million.

In 2020, PC sales were 275 million units according to research company Gartner, 297 million according to Canalyst, and 302 million according to International Data Corp. (IDC). Subsequently, Gartner raised its 2020 estimate of PC sales to 309 million, and in January 2022, it estimated that PC sales in 2021 would be about 340 million.

IDC noted, "Demand is pushing the PC market forward and all signs indicate the surge has a way to go."

Further, IDC has developed a forecast of PC sales over the next five years, predicting sales of 357 million in 2021 and growing from there at 3 percent a year to 2025.

All this data suggests a significant resurgence of PC sales is under way.

We have identified four software developments that might underlie this resurgence.

The Cloud

The first development is known as the cloud.

In his latest book, *Thank You for Being Late*, published in 2016, Thomas Friedman analyzes accelerating forces that are reshaping our world in the twenty-first century, impacting each one of us. He describes the accelerating forces and presents suggestions on changes that we as individuals and collectively could make to cope with them.

Friedman identifies three fields in which the rates of innovations are accelerating: computer technology, globalisation, and the environment.

The starting point of his analysis is the incredible increases in the number of transistors on a microchip that have occurred over the last four decades, in accordance with Moore's law, that the power of the microchip will double every two years. These microchips are used as the brains of personal computers.

This progress in chip technology is driving the accelerating power of computers, but Freidman says it is matched by accelerating improvements in four other key components of computers: memory, networking, software applications, and the sensors feeding data to the computer. Putting together the improvements in all five of these components has allowed a new service to be offered: the cloud, which is taking computing to a new level of capacity.

Cloud services, we suggest, may lead to the next major boost in PC sales.

Freidman claims that cloud services are so important an advance that it deserves a bigger name, and he calls it a supernova. In his book, he describes it this way:

> This technological supernova just keeps releasing energy at an exponentially accelerating rate—because all the critical components are being driven down in cost and up in performance at a Moore's Law exponential rate. This release of energy is enabling the reshaping of

virtually every man-made system that modern society
is built on.[60]

Freidman gives several examples to illustrate the power of this
supernova. Here are two:

The first is in the field of design. Tom Wujec is with Autodesk,
a global leader in 3D design, which offers software to design many
different objects, from buildings to cars to medical instruments. He
headed up a design team tasked with building a prototype dinosaur for
the Royal Ontario Museum in Toronto, from a huge, recovered fossil.
The project was completed, and the model was very successful; but it
took over two years and cost over five hundred thousand dollars.

Some years later, Wujec dropped in on the museum and saw his
dinosaur and wondered whether the same model could be made with
modern design software tools. Using a cloud app called 123D Catch, in
less than an hour's work, Wujec used a smartphone to convert photos
he took of the original model to produce a digital 3D model that was
better than the original. To Wujec, this was just an example of how "all
industries are becoming computable," allowing designers incredible new
power and speed for their work.

A second example concerns Walmart's effort to compete with
Amazon in the retail world of e-commerce, taking advantage of the
power of Friedman's supernova. In 2011, after failed attempts to create
a system that would be competitive with Amazon, Walmart developed
a mobile app to be used by its customers to search for a product, pay
for its purchase, and arrange for delivery of the product from a nearby
Walmart store or a Walmart fulfillment center. To develop this app,
Walmart exploited the advances embodied in the supernova, using
Hadoop software to handle big, distributed databases, and GitHub to
access the immense library of retail software now available.

These are but two of many examples of how the power of the cloud
(Friedman's supernova) is being used to create innovations in a wide
variety of industries.

---

[60] Thomas Friedman, *Thank You for Being Late.*

The Evans Strategic Communications Group provides rankings of the top cloud providers by revenue in its CloudWars Rankings.

Its top rankings for calendar 2019 showed Microsoft as number 1, with revenue of $44.7 billion, followed by Amazon AWS with $34.8 billion, IBM with $21.2 billion, Salesforce with $17.1 billion, and Google with $8.9 billion.

> Microsoft had just overtaken the number 1 spot from the leader for several years, Amazon's AWS. According to CloudWars, Microsoft is now growing faster than AWS (39 percent annually over 37 percent). IBM's growth rate is substantially less at 14 percent but has improved in 2019.

> Further, a survey of chief information officers shows Microsoft's Azure is now more popular than AWS.

Microsoft Management Changes

In 2014, Satya Nadella succeeded Steve Ballmer as the CEO of Microsoft. Prior to his appointment, he was the executive vice president of Microsoft's Cloud and Enterprise Group. A major focus of Nadella's regime has been the steady improvement and expansion of Azure, Microsoft's Cloud services.

In the 2019 annual report, Nadella explained why Azure has been so successful.

Microsoft has a strong focus on the needs of its customers. "Our mission [is] to empower every person and every organization on the planet to achieve more.

"Today, every company is a technology company, and every organization will increasingly need to build its own proprietary technology solutions to compete and grow.

"Today, 95% of the Fortune 500 trust Azure for their mission critical workloads."

Microsoft's strong focus on its customers needs and, in particular, the growing initiatives to ensure trustworthiness of its cloud services, are major reasons why it is forging to the lead in cloud services.

IBM

IBM was the early leader in providing cloud services. But it lost that lead, first to Amazon's AWS and, in recent years, to Microsoft's Azure.

IBM's mission throughout its life was established by Thomas Watson to be the provider of "BIG Solutions to the problems of Big Business with innovative technology." This is still its mission, and it has served it well through the years. It has allowed IBM to establish a dominant position in providing technology services to big business and to build a virtually impregnable moat around this business, which has held up until recently. Today, there are signs of leaks in the moat. "We think IBM's moat is deteriorating as the Cloud transition chips away at IBM's competitive advantage associated with customer switching costs [the cost and disruption of changing from one supplier to another]," writes Morningstar's Julie Sharma.

Nevertheless, there is some hope that IBM may be again righting the ship. On October 28, 2018, IBM announced the acquisition of Red Hat, "the world's leading provider of open-source cloud software."

In April 2020, IBM announced changes in its leadership: Arvid Krishna, the architect of the Red Hat purchase and boss of Big Blue's Cloud and Cognitive Software unit, became CEO, and James Whitehurst, CEO of Red Hat, became the president of IBM. We see these steps as strong indicators of the importance to IBM of the acquisition of Red Hat.

Since the days of Lou Gerstner in the 1990s, IBM has been dedicated to "opening the stack" and embracing open-source computer technology. Red Hat is a leader in this aspect of cloud computing. IBM believes that its acquisition will greatly strengthen IBM's cloud services. There is an indication that began happening in 2019, when IBM's cloud revenue was $21.2 billion and grew at a 14 percent rate. While this was well below the growth rates of AWS and Azure, it represents a turnaround at IBM, and more may be expected in future years.

A major concern of enterprises using cloud services is privacy and security. A skit by Kitty Flanagan, an Australian comedian, provides an amusing take on the importance of security in the cloud.

Bob Evans, the creator of CloudWars, a site dedicated to reporting developments in cloud services, has a more skeptical take on IBM's cloud prospects. In 2017, the CloudWars ranking of the top ten most influential cloud vendors ranked IBM in seventh position, well behind the two leaders, Microsoft's Azure and Amazon's AWS. In reviewing the new IBM CEO's plans for the cloud, CloudWars notes that IBM's major competitors are making sweeping and disruptive changes in the way they deliver their cloud services and wonders if IBM can keep pace, given its longstanding and apparently dysfunctional operating structure.

"In too many cases over the past several years, IBM has watched a parade of other tech vendors—almost always smaller, quicker, more focused and more able to deliver timely and more-relevant solutions and experiences—cut into its business and either sever or weaken its long-standing client relationships."

By looking at the CloudWars, in 2021, we can see that cloud services of all types continue to boom. In his March 14, 2022, report, Evans lists the top ten providers of cloud services. On his list for the second quarter of 2021:

Microsoft's Azure is number one with cloud revenues of $19.5 billion.
Amazon's AWS is number two with $14.8 billion.
Google Cloud is number three with $4.3 billion.
Salesforce is number four with $6.3 billion.
SAP is number five with $2.7 billion.
Oracle is number six with $2.5 billion.
IBM is number ten with $7 billion.

The ranking of IBM as tenth seems to be an error. Based on cloud service sales, IBM ranks third in 2021. It appears that the acquisition of Red Hat in 2019 and accompanying changes in leadership at IBM is having a significant positive effect on its cloud sales.

The cloud, as predicted by Thomas Friedman in *Thank You for Being Late*, is growing quickly, because cloud services transfer the job of maintaining critical software to the software experts, ensuring software is up to date, more economical, and high quality. We suggest that this cloud attractiveness could create a push for more PCs as access devices.

Advances in Artificial Intelligence

A second possible driver of PC sales may be advances in artificial intelligence (AI). A *Time Special Edition* termed it "The Future of Mankind."

In 1956, a small group of mathematicians and scientists met at Dartmouth College to explore the possibilities of machine learning. The group is generally credited with inventing the term "artificial intelligence," although the seeds of what they were after were established much earlier. As they put it, "Every aspect of learning or any other feature of intelligence can in principle be so precisely described that a machine can be made to simulate it.

"Almost all the hallmarks of our current technological moment— talkative digital personal assistants like Siri and Alexa, genomic-research breakthroughs, instantaneous language translations, self driving cars— have at their foundation one key, if broad, thing in common: Artificial Intelligence, or A.I."[61]

Geoffrey Hinton and Neural networks

The big AI breakthrough came not through the application of mathematical rules of logic, but by the simulation of a different learning system: neural networks.

---

[61] *Time Magazine Special Edition on Artificial Intelligence.*

Neural networks in humans and animals reach conclusions by optimizing patterns developed from examples. This is essentially how young children learn before their capacity for deductive reasoning has been developed. They learn from observing repeated examples and using their neural networks to deduce patterns in the examples and to learn that if a certain pattern is repeated often enough, they can generalize a conclusion.

To take a simple example, suppose a child is told repeatedly that eating broccoli is good for you because it is a green food, but eating cauliflower is not. After enough iterations, the child will learn that it should eat broccoli, but not cauliflower, and store this conclusion in its memory. The process by which it reaches this conclusion is not deductive logic but the application of its neural networks. The neural networks allow the child to develop a conclusion from the examples given to train it. This is different from the process of deductive reasoning used by adults. Of course, adults use both systems of reasoning to develop their own library of conclusions.

Researchers have learned how to simulate neural networks using special mathematical formulas or recursive algorithms "to learn discrete tasks by identifying patterns in large amount of data."[62]

The whole field of artificial intelligence received a boost with the continued increases in power of the computer and the development of access to big data sets, facilitated by such developments as the growth of cloud computing. These developments allow the accessing of large samples of data, thousands and millions of data, and the processing of these data sets by powerful computers. This capability simulates the brain's neural networks to construct more and more reliable and accurate conclusions, just as the human brain does.

The current developments of artificial intelligence are proceeding in many research centers around the world, and one of the leaders in these developments is Geoffrey Hinton at the University of Toronto.

As a November 2017 *New York Times* article put it, "Mr. Hinton, a professor, built a system that could analyze thousands of photos and

---

[62] Ibid.

teach itself to identify common objects like flowers and cars with an accuracy that didn't seem possible." The technique that Hinton used was the simulation of a neural network.

Currently, Hinton is exploring an advance using an alternative mathematical technique that he calls a Capsule Network. The neural network he developed has limitations: "If a neural network is trained on images that show a coffee cup from only one side, it is unlikely to recognize a coffee cup turned upside down." Hinton's new system will use a different mathematical technique that operates in three dimensions, not just two. This will allow much more complex conclusions to be developed from masses of examples. Hinton hopes that this new approach will allow computers to deliver the kinds of autonomous instruments that will improve the efficiency of voice-recognition instruments and improve such projects as driverless cars.

Artificial intelligence is currently expanding its reach to many diverse fields, such as medical diagnosis and treatment optimization, robotic manufacturing, military applications, astronomy, and beyond. The PC may be the device that people use to access the AI, and perhaps one day, they'll use it to carry out AI simulations of neural networks.

Artificial intelligence, as we know it today, has its limitations. In a December 28, 2017, article in Canada's *Financial Post*, Claire Boswell noted, "AI systems are now much better than humans at identifying patterns in large amounts of data, [but] the machines inability to use common sense or generalize means they can't do much beyond the scope of one narrow task. … Artificial intelligence has a long way to go before it can replace most human employees. … Little progress has been made in replicating general intelligence."

Nevertheless, the ongoing advances in AI and the pervasiveness of it may be helping to drive PC sales.[63]

---

[63] Peter Farwell, *Artificial Intelligence and the Job Market.*

Big Data

This is our third choice for a technological advance that may increase PC sales.

The term "big data" has slightly different meanings for different purposes. For our purposes, it means the masses of digital information or data coming into internet-connected users from multiple types of connected devices. These devices were primarily PCs in the 1990s, but now include smartphones, tablets, web servers, and other devices. The amounts of data streaming into users increases daily. Much of this data is unstructured and expressed in natural language. Massive systems of networked mainframes are needed to deal with this large amount of information. More importantly, an array of software and services are needed to collect this data and store it in a secure and reliable environment, in a manner that can be accessed for analysis.

For purposes of determining the potential impact on sales of PCs, we note that there will be a need for access devices. The personal computer would seem to be ideal for this purpose. The PC has a large screen capable of displaying written words, tables, or graphs. It also has increasing amounts of processing power, so it can be used to analyze data provided from servers and mainframes. These capabilities would seem to make it the premier access device for extracting valuable information from big data sets.

The Internet of Things (IOT)

A fourth area of current technological advance is the Internet of Things.

The concept of IOT has been around for some years. British entrepreneur Kevin Ashton first used the term in 1999 to refer to a global network of radio frequency transmitters embedded in a variety of things. Today, it refers to an internet-connected network of physical devices of all types, equipped with embedded sensors and capable of transmitting the sensed information wirelessly to the internet and from there to a variety of computers, smartphones, and the like, to be stored, analyzed, and used to control the physical devices remotely.[64]

"In the consumer market, IoT technology is most synonymous with products pertaining to the smart home, including devices and appliances (such as lighting fixtures, thermostats, home security systems and cameras)."[65]

The potential appears to be immense. It is estimated by Gartner that there were over 3.8 billion internet-connected "things" at the end of 2015. In 2014, ABI Research estimated that over 40 billion things would be wirelessly connected to the internet and feeding it with all sorts of sensed information by 2020.

In 2018, Cisco's chairman, John Chambers, forecast that within five years, there would be 50 billion connected things in a market worth $19 trillion.

In a *Toronto Globe and Mail* report on business article, Alec Scott described the current and potential applications of the Internet of Things. He noted that "these intelligent machines are already altering spheres as diverse as health care, manufacturing, city planning, transportation and power generation, agriculture and household management." And further, that the devices themselves are "causing macro shifts in how we live and work."

In his article, Scott detailed a long list of Internet of Things applications in play today, in such fields as home heat and light controls; traffic light controls; manufacturing automation and defect prevention; robotic cars (such as the Tesla), planes, and trains; safety; health and fitness assistance; management of power grids; and farming.

Scott also noted that there are several obstacles still to be overcome, involving issues such as standardization of computer languages, security, privacy, and preventing hackers from taking subversive control of things, as well as legal issues about who owns the information and regulatory issues.

---

[64] Wikipedia, Internet of Things.

[65] Ibid.

In 2018, IBM announced a $3 billion program of R&D focussed on the Internet of Things. One would expect a lot of this would be aimed at developing the infrastructure for the Internet of Things. IBM is already partnering with many companies targeting specific areas of the Internet of Things.

In a recent report examining technology adoption trends by cities, Forrester Research, Inc. cited IBM for its full set of smart city solution components, making IBM one of only two vendors that is truly a smart city service provider.

In 2018, IBM was very actively focused on developing the Internet of Things and had been for some time. But there are big and tough competitors pursuing the same opportunity. These include Cisco, the giant computer networking systems leader, Siemens, and other longtime manufacturers of control systems, such as Honeywell International. Still, if the forecasters are right, this is a huge opportunity, and clear leaders have yet to emerge.

This may also be an opportunity for the personal computer. The PC could be used as a device that receives all the new data, analyzes it, and directs the use of the analysis. But this will require the development of new application software to carry out these functions for different industries.

An example of the type of software innovation we have in mind is the Event Stream Processing system offered by Statistical Analysis Systems (SAS).

Statistical Analysis Systems was started in 1976 in North Carolina with an assignment to produce a software system that would analyze agricultural information to improve the efficiency of farm management. It grew quickly to help clients in many industries, such as pharmaceuticals, financial institutions, education, and government.[66] The rapid growth of SAS over the next few decades was in part due to the fact its software ran across all platforms, "using the multivendor architecture for which it is known today."[67]

---

[66] SAS Website: SAS.com.

[67] Ibid.

In response to the development of the Internet of Things, SAS offers a system called Event Stream Processing to receive the mass of data from the Internet of Things, analyze and store the data, and release it in real time for use in managing the system of things producing the data. SAS describes the opportunities presented by the Internet of Things this way:

"The large array of connected devices [the Internet of Things] is delivering an array of new data from the sensors contained in the Internet of Things.

"This data offers the promise of new services, improved efficiency and, possibly, more competitive business models."[68]

The SAS Event Stream Processing was designed with this opportunity in mind.

As an example of the SAS Event Stream system at work, Manheim, the European automotive remarketer, used it to transform its business and increase its market share over a two-year operation. Manheim is the largest remarketer of vehicles worldwide, auctioning 10 million vehicles a year. Manheim wanted to improve the way it integrates, analyzes, and exploits the mass of data it draws in its business, from car auctions, to enhance the experience of auto dealers (its customers). Among other things, it used SAS Enterprise Guide to make it easy to use SAS in a Windows environment.

For its transformation, Manheim needed to quickly analyze and model large volumes of data about the 10 million cars it auctions every year and the thousands of dealers that use its services. It wanted to realign its dealer network to improve performance, so the dealers could see where a particular model was achieving the best price and used the analysis of the mass of data to accomplish this.

The resulting realignment of the dealer network has been a resounding success: a 17 percent increase in the dealer market over two years and a 15 percent increase in dealer volume.

Both the general outline of the SAS Event Stream system and the Manheim example suggest several opportunities for use of PCs in the system.

---

[68] Ibid.

In 2018, expectations were that there would be a very large and extensive growth in the number of connected things. ABI estimated that by 2020, there would be over 40 billion things wirelessly connected to the internet. As noted above, Cisco's chairman, John Chambers, had forecast that within five years, there would be 50 billion connected things in a market worth $19 trillion.

These forecasts have not been realized.

Perhaps more specifically, as we saw above, in 2018, IBM announced a $3 billion R&D program focused on the Internet of Things. IBM also announced a series of partnerships aimed at specific fields of the Internet of Things. However, in IBM's 2020 annual report to shareholders, there is not one mention of the Internet of Things. (IBM's efforts in 2020 were focused on the cloud and artificial intelligence.)

As noted, people have raised concerns about privacy protection and security in the Internet of Things. As well, there are concerns about the lack of standardization and legal issues about who owns the information generated. The combination of these issues may well be slowing down the spread of the Internet of Things. Nevertheless, it is an area of technology in which the PC could be used as an access and controlling device. It bears watching as the various concerns are minimized or eliminated.

Summary of Current Developments

In these four areas of current technological advancement, the PC could become the primary access device. This will require the development of application software, such as SAS's Event Stream system, that can be best used on personal computers. For this to happen, the PC will have to beat very tough competition from the smartphone set and newer devices such as the voice-activated devices being brought onto the market today.

Comparison of Personal Computers and Smartphones

The PC has a clear advantage for handling large amounts of information and managing information. The greater processing power and large screen make it the primary device for dealing with spreadsheets, graphs, pictures, videos, and larger text documents. It will continue to be used by writers and other creators, editors, publishers, and readers of text, graphs, and charts. On the other hand, it is not mobile, less convenient to use, harder to use, and slower to use than smartphones and tablets.

These devices will require new application software to enable them to be used as access devices for either information in the cloud or for data coming from the Internet of Things. The development of this software will likely determine which devices will dominate in this field.

Newer Devices

In 2017, new forms of competitors came out for the function of digital access devices. Google introduced home management devices, Google Home and Google Home Mini, that are entirely voice activated. Apple brought out its own home management device, HomePod, that is also voice activated. Voice-activation systems are improving in leaps and bounds. Some people believe they will replace typing systems entirely. These dedicated devices will pose tough competition for the PCs as digital access devices.

Heavy Users of Personal Computers, Including Laptops

Another perspective on potential future use of personal computers is to look at who the heavy PC users are today and who is likely to use them in the future.

In general, we would think the heavy users are professionals and analysts creating documents, tables, and graphs using word processors, such as Word, spreadsheet software, such as Excel, and presentation aid producers, such as PowerPoint. In other words, the people who are using the old mega apps. These users would include businesspeople, office workers, lawyers, accountants, engineers, doctors, architects, and so on.

It also includes students and teachers, sales personnel, writers, and journalists. All these people have been heavy PC users and seem likely to continue to do so. This will be particularly true if innovations come that make the PC easier to use.

For example, we can see that artificial intelligence is continually improving voice-recognition capabilities, such as Siri and Alexa. One can imagine that at some point, dictation to a digital personal assistant will replace typing. This is already happening with younger generations.

Just for Fun: Market Caps

Just for fun, let's look at the market caps of our stars and a few other corporations. The stock market value of a corporation's shares is a good measure of how successfully the business has been managed.

Here is a list showing market values at December 31, 2021:

Company	Market Value
Apple	$2.913 trillion
Microsoft	$2.512 trillion
Google	$1.951 trillion
IBM	$117 billion
Amazon	$1.691 trillion
Facebook	$932 billion
Tesla	$1.071 trillion
GM	$83 billion
Saudi Aramco	$1.900 trillion
Intel	$206 billion
Berkshire Hathaway	$660 billion

We can see that Apple is in the lead by a good margin. We attribute that to the exceptional management under Tim Cook, who continues to build the Apple ecosystem of dedicated users. Apple is the leader in smartphone sales, and the iMac recently moved up into the top five personal computers. Intuitiveness and ease of use have been features of Apple products from the beginning under Steve Jobs, and this continues today. For example, the steady stream of new and improved iPhones, now in the thirteenth iteration, have been designed to make it almost automatic to switch to the latest version. Apple has well earned its leadership position.

In second place is Microsoft. This position too has been well earned, as Microsoft has been rejuvenated under the leadership of Satya Nadella, who has focussed the firm on successfully building a leadership position in cloud services.

Google has come on strong in recent years by building on the fact that it has the dominant search engine. It has also invested its surplus cash flow on research and development in a manner that encourages creativity in building new services. We expect this success to be continued.

To show that these leadership positions are no fluke, we show the following table of market caps over the last eleven years:

Market values of technology leaders' stock

market values of technology leaders stock											
	2011	2012	2013	2014	2015	2016	2017	2018	2019	2020	2021
Company	Dec.31 Values in billions of dollars										
Apple	377	500	501	643	583	609	861	746	1290	2250	2913
Microsoft	218	224	310	382	440	483	660	780	1200	1681	2512
Google				60	528	539	729	723	921	1185	1951
IBM	218	214	198	159	133	158	142	101	119	112	117
Amazon	79	113	183	144	318	356	563	737	920	1185	1691
Facebook		63	139	217	297	332	513	374	585	778	932
Tesla	3	4	19	28	32	34	52	57	76	669	1071
GM	32	39	61	56	51	53	58	47	51	60	83
Saudi Aramco									1878	2050	1900
Berkshire Hathaway	189	221	292	371	325	402	489	502	552	544	660
Intel	123	102	129	172	163	172	216	212	257	194	206
Dow Jones (est)	12045	13000	16500	17800	1770	19100	24300	25500	28000	29600	36700

We can see from the Dow Jones that the eleven-year period of our table has been one of the longest bull markets in stock market history. The last two years mark an exceptional period due to the pandemic and the period when governments around the world have been living under Modern Monetary Theory (MMT), a controversial economic theory. MMT argues that a government that can print its own currency should not worry about deficits, at least until inflation rears its ugly head. While the subject is debated, MMT has carried the day in the last few years, at least until 2022, and one of the beneficiaries has been the stock market. Nevertheless, our technology stars have performed above even these stimulants.

Conclusion

In this book, we have shown how Robert Noyce and Gordon Moore, accompanied by Andy Groves, invented the microprocessor, the computer chip, that became the CPU, the core of the personal computer.

Ed Roberts at MITS built the first PC kit.

Steve Jobs and Steve Wozniak developed the Apple I and Apple II to create the early personal computers.

Dan Bricklin and Bob Frankston built VisiCalc, the first spreadsheet for the PC, that made the Apple II a useful tool for business.

Bill Gates and Paul Allen built the operating system for the IBM PC and clones, and obtained control of the PC industry.

Seymour Rubenstein created WordStar, the first really good word processor for the personal computer, and understood how it would make the PC useful to the masses.

Michael Dell became the leader in PC sales.

A group of innovators established the standards required to make the public internet work.

Mark Andreesen created the first web browser.

Sergei Brin and Larry Page, with the business guidance of Eric Schmidt, made Google Chrome the search engine of choice.

Jeff Bezos made the internet a disrupter of retail commerce.

Mark Zuckerberg took the social media giant, Facebook (recently renamed as Meta), to a new level of popularity.

Michael Lazaridis and Jim Balsillie developed the BlackBerry, the first smartphone.

Steve Jobs retuned to Apple and created the Apple iPhone, which became highly popular with consumers.

Satya Nadella led Microsoft to become the leading cloud service provider.

Steve Jobs and Tim Cook rejuvenated the Apple ecosystem and made Apple the most valuable company in the world.

Positive Things to Watch For

Improvements in the speed of operation and ease of use of the PC, to match those of the smartphones, including more intuitive aids and mega apps.

Exciting new applications. We have suggested four areas in which new applications could prosper: the Internet of Things, the cloud, artificial intelligence, and big data. The PC could be used as the primary access device for developments in all these areas.

Continued lowering of costs and improvements in speed.

Tribute

We are deeply indebted to the pioneers who, time and time again, showed that where there is a will, there is a way and put the personal computer at the center of the digital technology revolution.

References

Peter Farwell, *The Personal Computer, Past, Present and Future.*

Wikipedia, www.wikipedia.com

Walter Isaacson, *Steve Jobs* (2011).

Steve Wozniak, *iWoz: Computer Geek to Cult Icon, An Autobiography* (2006).

Brian Kernighan, *D is for Digital* (2012).

George Gilder, *Telecosm* (2000).

Dave Kinnaman and LouAnn Ballew, *Network Essentials* (1999).

Frank Derfler and Les Freed, *How Networks Work* (1993).

Peter Clemente, *The State of the Net: The New Frontier* (1998).

Behrouz Forouzan, *Introduction to Data Communications and Networking* (1998).

Daniel Minoli, *Internet & Intranet Engineering.*

Walter Isaacson, *The Innovators* (2014).

Thomas Friedman, *Thank You for Being Late* (2016).

David Vise, *The Google Story* (2018).

Ben Mezrich, *The Accidental Billionaires* (2009).

Margaret O'Mara, *The Code: Silicon Valley and the Remaking of America.*

Appendix A

Personal Computer Sales in the
Pre-Internet Era (in thousands of units)

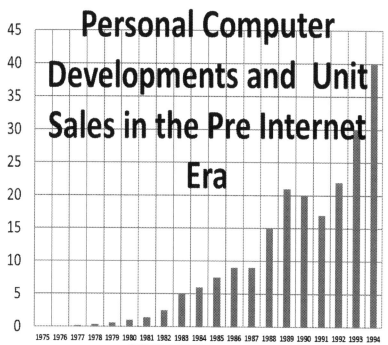

Personal Computer Developments and Unit Sales in the Pre Internet Era

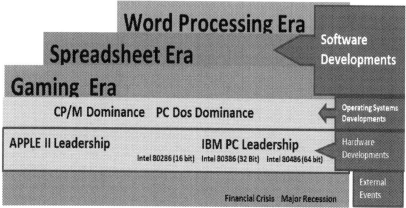

Appendix B

A Hierarchy of Computer Hardware and Software

Name of Layer	A Hierarchy of Computer Hardware and Software Function
Hardware	Tangible computing devices and peripherals.
Transistor	An electronic switch that can turn currents on and off, like a light switch.
Circuits	Wires that connect the transistors and other components of a computer system, sometimes called buses.
Logic Gate	The fundamental building block of a computer. An electronic gate made up of a group of transistors that creates a single output signal (current) based on one or two input signals.
Integrated Circuits	Groups of logic gates and interconnecting wiring on a single, small sheet of silicon or chip.

CPU	Central processing unit that runs the arithmetic and logical computations, controls the sequence of operations, and moves data within the computer and to and from components.
RAM	Electronic memory that can be randomly and quickly accessed and changed by the CPU, memory that is used to store both active programs and data needed by them. Memory that disappears when power is turned off.
Secondary Storage	Internal disk or hard drive, external storage devices such as DVDs, optical storage disks, and flash memory devices that store data and programs permanently for access by the CPU more slowly than RAM.
Input Devices	Keyboards, mice, microphones, scanners, that provide input to the CPU.
Output Devices	Monitor, screens, printers, and so on that take output from the CPU.
Software	Computers are binary processors that store and process discrete data represented by a binary system. All data and instructions must be represented in binary form, a series of ones and zeros rather than in analog or continuous form. This system is usually referred to as digital as opposed to continuous data.
Bits	The basic representation of data as a binary digit, a number that is either a one or a zero, corresponding to a transistor switch that is either on or off.

Bytes	A group of eight bits that allows 256 (2 to the 8th power) different pieces of data to be represented in binary form.
	Bytes can be combined to represent a wide range of distinct data, such as colours or symbols in other languages.
ASCII	The American Standard Code for Information Interchange that prescribes what basic data is represented by a particular byte, data such as letters of the alphabet, both in upper- and lowercase, digits, punctuation, and mathematical and logical operations. In the beginning, computers were programmed in ASCII, which was referred to as machine language. In time, programmers began to use ordinary language to express computer instructions, such as ADD rather than a symbol such as +. Other programmers developed short routines to carry out standard functions such as sorting and filing. The programming language that encompassed these developments was called Assembly language. The process of converting from Assembly language to machine language was done by software called assemblers. An Assembly language is unique to each type of CPU.
Specific Programming Languages	New languages were developed for specific uses. Fortran was developed to simplify programming of mathematical calculations. COBOL was developed for processing business transactions such as inventory, management, and payroll.

BASIC	The Beginners All-purpose Symbolic Instruction Code (BASIC) was developed as a simple, easy-to-learn and -use system. It was used to program the early PCs.
C and C++	C and C++ were higher level, general-purpose programming languages independent of any particular CPU. They were developed to make programming easier and safer. They are used to write most widely used software in plain language. Programs written in these languages are translated to the Assembly language of a specific CPU by a compiler. This in turn is translated into the machine binary code of ones and zeroes by an Assembler program.
Operating Systems	Operating systems are the software programs that manage and control all the operations of a computer. Their tasks include managing the CPU operations, scheduling and coordinating different tasks, managing both the RAM and secondary memory (the file system), and managing the peripheral devices by device drivers. The first operating system for the IBM PC was known as CP/M. it was followed by PC-DOS (also known as MS-DOS). The most common operating systems for computers today are Windows, UNIX, LINUX, and Mac OS. They provide a standardized platform of services, such as storing and retrieval of data in memory, for application programs.

Libraries	Libraries are software programs that provide generic services, such as date and time references, used in various applications.
Application Software	Applications are software programs, such as Word or Excel, that perform specific tasks for the user. They may be as complicated as Word, programmed in C++, or as simple as a specific calculation, programmed in Java script.
	The above hierarchy was compiled with reference to the descriptions in Brian Kernighan's *D for Digital,* with some variations.

Appendix C

Personal Computer Sales in the Start of the Internet Era, in Thousands

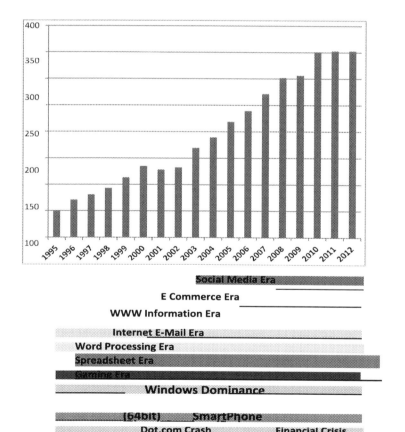

Appendix D

A Hierarchy of Network Hardware and Software

Hardware

Computers
In this case, intelligent communication devices, such as a personal computer, smartphone, or tablet.

Network Interface Card (NIC)
A circuit board or chip inside a computer, through which the computer connects to a network.
The NIC has one or more ports from which a network cable connects the computer to a network.

Network Cable
The cable, also called the physical medium, that carries a data signal over the network; it may be a telephone twisted pair line, a cable company's coaxial cable, a fiber optic cable, or a wireless network.

Modem
A network connector that converts digital signals into analog signals and vice versa.

ISP Cable
The cable connecting a network, owned and maintained by an Internet Service Provider.

LAN (Local Area Network)	Generally, a private network connecting computers to various devices, such as printers, modems, and routers that connect the private network to the internet.
Online Information Server	Private companies, such as AOL, CompuServe, Microsoft MSN, that provide internet connection services.
ISP (Internet Service Provider)	Today, typically a telephone or cable company, but also includes the online information servers.
Bridge, Router, Gateway	Network management computers that relay data from one network to another.
Internet Backbone Network	Typically, fiber optic cable spanning cities, countries, and oceans to link LANs and other networks to form the internet.
Website	A computer connected to the internet that provides information for other internet users.

Software

Operating System	A software program, such as Microsoft's Windows, that manages a computer.
Web Browsers	Application programs that allow a user on a connected computer to go out into the internet to communicate with websites on the internet and to obtain data from those websites.
Email Systems	Application programs that allow a user on a connected computer to send text messages to and from other connected computers.
	A standards system called MIME embedded in email software allows the inclusion of graphics, photographs, and videos in an email.

124

Appendix E

A Hierarchy of Network Standards (Protocols)

Internet Protocols

The internet is a universal electronic network that permits the transfer of data between computers and between networks of computers.

Internet protocols are universal standards governing the movement of data from one computer to another over the internet. Without these standards, it would be impossible to communicate between the many different types of computers and networks.

The internet is a "dumb" network; all the "intelligence" is in the software on the computers transferring data over the internet. This differs from the telephone network, in which the telephone terminals are dumb and the intelligence is in the network.

Domain Name System

The Domain Name System (DNS) sets out a hierarchy of names for computers accessing the internet. The top level names the type of organization or country of the computer, while lower levels provide increasingly specific names of networks and computers.

The DNS system provides names used at the application layer.

IP Address

IP addresses are 32- or 64-bit sets of hexadecimal (16) numbers that provide the physical layer addresses for each network server and computer connected to the internet. Assignment of IP addresses is also managed by ICANN.

There is a one-to-one correlation between domain names and IP addresses, although they are assigned in slightly different ways.

Routing

Routers are computers that connect networks and select the route to get a data packet from one computer through the different networks to the receiving computer, using information in the data packet's envelope, added at the network layer of the OSI network protocols.

Routers are continually talking to one another to identify the best routes for particular data sets and store the information in their routing tables.

ISO

The International Standards Organization, formed in 1947 to establish global agreement on communication standards.

| **OSI Model** | Open Systems Interconnection Model, a seven-layer set of standards for design of network systems, that permit communication across all types of computer networks. Each layer sets out standards for a segment of the process of moving data across and between networks, from one computer to another, regardless of the physical equipment, the programming language, platform, operating system, application, or user interface. (See *Network Essentials*, 109.)
|

The first three layers define the network; the next four layers define the message and the connection.

| **The Physical Layer** | The physical layer sets the standards that allow the different physical components of the network to transmit a bit stream from sender to receiver.
|

This layer defines the mechanical and electrical specifications for the primary physical connections, the number of connector pins, and the function of each pin between the connecting cables, whether twisted pair, coaxial cable, fiber optic cable, or wireless connection.

It permits the transmission of a stream of zeros and ones over the network in the form of electrical signals.

Datalink layer	This layer defines standards for delivering data packets through each segment of the network without error. The datalink layer is specific to each part of the larger network. It takes a data packet from the network layer and adds addressing and other control information to form a frame. The frame is passed to the physical layer, where it is converted to zeros and ones for transmission.
Network Layer	The network layer sets the standards allowing the data communication packets to be switched (creating temporary connections between physical links) from one link to the next until the packet reaches its intended destination.
	It converts logical names and addresses to physical addresses and handles transmission problems such as congestion.
Transport Layer	This layer sets the standards that allow a complete data message to be delivered. It divides a message into packets for transmission and reassembles them at the destination. It also provides for error recognition and recovery.
Session Layer	This layer provides standards for controlling a communication session between two application programs on different computers. It covers user name recognition, user authentication, logins, and security.

Presentation Layer   This layer translates data flow into a format usable by the application programs, and vice versa.

It also covers data compression and data encryption. It is specific to each type of computer or device.

Application Layer   This top layer enables the user to access the network through familiar application programs by providing standards for a variety of services such as email, remote file access and transfer, shared data base management, and other distributed information services.

These descriptions of the seven layers of the OSI Model were based on two sources: Behrouz Fourouzan, *Introduction to Data Communications and Networking*, chapter 3, and Dave Kinnaman and LouAnn Ballew, *Network Essentials*, chapter 9.

TCP/IP   TCP/IP is a set of protocols developed for transmissions of data over the internet.

It was originally created by the Advanced Research Project Agency (ARPA) of the US Department of Defense for ARPANET, a private packet-switched network of computers linked by third-party lines.

When the private ARPANET evolved into the public internet in the 1990s, the evolving TCP/IP standards became the protocols for the internet.

Under the TCP/IP standards, the internet operates like a single network, linking computers and other communication devices of all types.

Relationship to the Seven-Layer OSI Model

TCP/IP is a five-layer standards model that generally corresponds to the OSI model.

Physical and Datalink Layers

The TCP/IP model does not define standards for the physical or datalink layers of OSI. It works with all of the standards, including the OSI standards, for these two layers.

IP (the Internet Protocol)

The IP defines the standards for the network layer that govern how the network linking two computers is established and how individual packets are formatted and transmitted over that network.

It establishes a best-efforts delivery service that provides no error checking or tracking.

Each individual packet from the transport layer is enclosed at the IP network layer in an envelope called a datagram. The datagram has two parts:

(1) a header containing addressing and routing information, and (2) the data packet.

TCP **(the Transmission** **Control Protocol)**	TCP corresponds to the transport layer in the OSI model. It defines how communication data is divided into packets, how a connection over the internet is established between sending and receiving computers, how the packets are sent, and how they are reassembled at the receiving computer into the original data. It provides reliability and control functions.
Application Layer	This layer includes the functions of the session, presentation, and application layers of the OSI model. It sets out standards for establishing and managing a session (connection) between application programs on the sending and receiving computers, encompassing user authentication and other security features. It translates the communication data into a format usable by application programs in the sending and receiving computers, and provides data compression and encryption services. Finally, this top layer enables the user to access the network through familiar application programs, such as email programs. The following three protocol sets define the use of the internet for email communications.

SMTP	The Simple Mail Transfer Protocol (SMTP) sets the standards for email communication between computers. Typically, the email program is embedded in a browser, but it may also be a separate program, such as Microsoft's Outlook. The receiving computer is usually a server that is part of a software service, such as
	Yahoo, that stores the email until it is ready to be retrieved. There are two separate protocols for retrieving e- mails: POP and IMAP.
POP	The Post Office Protocol (POP) allows an email program to retrieve emails from a server and transfer them to a PC or other access device for reading and storage, while deleting the email on the server.
IMAP	The Internet Message Access Protocol (IMAP) allows the message on the server to be accessed from multiple devices, such as PCs, smartphones, and tablets without deleting the message on the server.

Appendix F

A History of Microsoft's PC Operating Systems

Windows 1.0 was the first in a succession of Windows PC operating systems that have allowed Microsoft to maintain its dominance in that field to present times. By 1996, Microsoft had obtained a 90 percent market share in PC operating systems.

In 1990, Windows 3.0 was released with an improved program manager and a new icon system that provided a better user interface, a new file manager, support for 16 colors, and greater speed and reliability.[69] Windows 3.0 was well received and sold over 2 million copies in half a year.[70]

In 1995, Windows 95 was released with greatly improved user-friendliness, as a result of the use of an Object-oriented user interface. It also introduced the Start menu and Taskbar to replace the Program manager. It too was well accepted.

In 1998, Windows 98 was introduced with a browser, Internet Explorer, built in.

---

[69] *Thought Magazine.*
[70] Wikipedia.

In 2000, Windows 2000 based on Microsoft's NT networking technology, was released, and included software updates over the internet.

In 2001, Windows XP was introduced, with better multimedia support and better performance.

In 2006, Windows Vista was released after a long development period. It contained a redesigned shell and user interface and significant technical changes, with a particular focus on security.[71]

In 2009, Windows 7 was released, incorporating various improvements, such as a better task bar and a home networking system.

In 2012, Windows 8 was introduced. It was an attempt to integrate the Windows PC Operating Systems with those for tablets and smartphones. It also was linked with other Microsoft services such as social media and game offerings. Generally, it was not well received by PC users.

In 2015, Windows 10 was released.[72] It was a significant improvement on Windows 8 that included the return of the Start Menu and other measures to improve the user experience.

In 2021, Windows 11 was released.

This lengthy list of versions incorporated enough improvements over the years to keep Windows as the dominant PC operating system.

---

[71] Wikipedia.
[72] Wikipedia.

Appendix G

A History of Developments that Led to the First Personal Computer

Walter Isaacson notes that the idea of a personal computer was envisioned by Vannevar Bush in 1945 while working at MIT. Bush was the "dean of the MIT school of Engineering, a founder of the electronics company Raytheon, and America's top military science advisor during World War II." In an article for *The Atlantic* magazine, Bush hypothesized a personal machine "that would store a person's words, pictures and other information." He named it the memex.

The idea of the memex (personal computing machine) was picked up by Douglas Engelbart, an engineer. Engelbart's focus was artificial intelligence, and he sought to create a machine like Bush's memex that would improve the intelligence of humans by supplementing it with the computing power of a personal computer.

In 1962, Engelbart published "Augmenting Human Intelligence," a paper describing his idea of computer-assisted human intelligence. He received a grant from Licklider at ARPA and went on to create his own Augmentation Research Center as part of the Stanford Research Institute.

One of Engelbart's first initiatives was the development of the "mouse," in an effort to find a simple way for humans to interact with a computing machine.

Engelbart developed a number of other features for his machine (dubbed the oNLine System) that ultimately became part of the personal computer. These included "on-screen graphics, multiple windows ... document sharing, email, instant messaging, hypertext linking, and the formatting of documents (among others)."

Engelbart linked up with Stewart Brand to demonstrate his oNLine System in December of 1968, in what was known as the "Mother of All Demos."

The next step toward the development of the personal computer was taken by Alan Kay. Kay attended the University of Utah, where he discovered a paper by Ivan Sutherland that described "Sketchpad: A Man-Machine, Graphical Communication System." Based on this idea, Kay envisioned "small personal computers with graphical displays easy enough for a kid to use and cheap enough for every individual to own." These computers would have "their own memory and processing power."

In 1970, Xerox Corp. created its own pure research center in Palo Alto, California, which became known as Xerox PARC. While at Xerox PARC, Kay wrote a paper describing his vision of "A Personal Computer for Children of All Ages." At PARC, Kay met Butler Lampson and Chuck Thacker, who agreed to build Kay's machine and produced a machine that was known as the Xerox Alto. The Alto had a bitmapped display in which each pixel on the monitor could be turned on and off individually.

It was operated by a combination of a mouse and keyboard, as Engelbart had envisioned. It was constructed in 1973. Xerox made thousands of Altos, but they were for use by Xerox employees and never sold to outsiders.

In 1975, Fred Moore, Gordon French, and Lee Felsenstein formed a club of innovators interested in building their own computers. This was the Homebrew Computer Club.

Appendix H

The Series of Intel Microchips

The following list sets out the history of the sequence of microchips, referred to as the "x86" chips, developed and manufactured by Intel that enabled it to fulfill Moore's Law for microchips for over four decades.

1971. Intel 4004 is released as first single-chip processor (a "computer on a chip"), with forty transistors.

1972. Intel 8008 is the first 8-bit microchip, substantially increasing processing speeds.

1974. Intel 8080 is the first true general-purpose microchip with 4,500 transistors and ten times the power of the 8008.

1975. Intel 8080 is used in the Altair 8800.

1978. Intel 8086 is the first 16-bit microchip.

1981. Intel 8088 is selected by IBM for IBM PC.

1982. Intel 80286 is released with 134,000 transistors.

1986. Intel 80386 is the first 32-bit microchip, with 275,000 transistors

1989. Intel i860 microchip is released with over 1 million transistors, to be used in supercomputers.

1992. Intel 80486 is introduced.

1993. Intel Pentium microchip with over 3,100,000 transistors is released.

1994. AMD dispute over licenses is settled by payment; Intel has right to clone 80386 chips.

1998. Intel Celeron chip is introduced for handheld devices.

1999. Intel Pentium chip is introduced.

2000. Intel Pentium 4 is introduced with 4 million transistors. This microchip had 100,000 times the number of transistors in the original 4004, which had forty transistors.

2003. Intel chip released for laptops.

2005. Apple agrees to use Intel chips in the Mac.

2006. Intel produces first quad-core processors.

2006. Intel is subject to several patent infringement and anti-competitive behavior suits.

2006–07. In October 2006, a lawsuit was filed by Transmeta against Intel for patent infringement on computer architecture and power efficiency technologies. The lawsuit was settled in October 2007, with Intel agreeing to pay $150 million initially and $20 million per year for the next five years. Both companies agreed to drop lawsuits against each other, while Intel was granted a nonexclusive license to use current and future patented Transmeta technologies in its chips for ten years.

2008. Intel Atom is released for netbooks.

In 2009, Intel settled a lawsuit by AMD for anti-competitive behavior for $1.2 billion.

2010. Intel Core family introduced. Intel Core is a line of mid- to high-end consumer, workstation, and enthusiast central processing units marketed by Intel. These processors displaced the existing mid- to high-end Pentium processors of the time, moving the Pentium to the entry level, and bumping the Celeron series of processors to the low end. Identical or more capable versions of Core processors are also sold as Xeon processors for the server and workstation markets.

The first Intel Core desktop processor—and typical family member—came from the Conroe iteration, a 65-nm dual-core design brought to market in July 2006, based on the all-new Intel Core microarchitecture with substantial enhancements in efficiency and performance; it outperformed the Pentium 4, while operating at drastically lower clock rates. The new substantial bump in microarchitecture came in November 2008, with the introduction of the 45-nm Bloomfield desktop processor on the Nehalem architecture, whose main advantage came from redesigned I/O and memory systems featuring the new Intel QuickPath Interconnect and an integrated memory controller.

Subsequent performance improvements have tended toward making additions rather than profound change, such as adding advanced vector management system instruction set extensions, first released in January 2011. Time has also brought improved support for virtualization and a trend toward higher levels of system integration and management functionality, through the ongoing evolution of facilities such as Intel's active management system.

2012. The Intel Xeon coprocessor is released.

2019. Intel releases the tenth generation of Core processors.

2020. Intel launches the eleventh generation of Core processors.

Printed in the United States
by Baker & Taylor Publisher Services